JUST
BILLA

MICHAEL O'CONNOR

MERCIER PRESS

MERCIER PRESS
5 French Church Street, Cork
16 Hume Street, Dublin 2

Trade enquiries to CMD DISTRIBUTION,
55a Spruce Avenue, Stillorgan Industrial Park, Blackrock, Dublin

ISBN 1 85635 295 1

10 9 8 7 6 5 4 3 2 1

TO MY WIFE NELL

ACKNOWLEDGEMENTS
We would like to thank the following for the use of their photographs: Tony
O'Connell, Mike English, William Whyte and *The Examiner*.

Printed in Ireland by Colour Books Ltd.

JUST BILLA

CONTENTS

FOREWORD

Billa is the Christy Ring of Cork comedy. I believe that nobody can do it better than Billa. Fifty years doing pantomime, and he is still in demand. He is still wanted by his very own.

I'm delighted to have had the opportunity to write about this unique Cork character. In all these stories and incidents that happened to himself, and many others, Billa captures the tone and sharpness of wit that can be heard in the streets of Cork every day. Even West Cork humour comes in for analysis. But I must also say, behind his humour and endless energy, there is also a very humble sensitive man, with an extraordinary gift of understanding children. The pantomime stage is really Billa doing what he loves best.

I want to thank sincerely his wife, Nell, and members of his family for their assistance; my own wife, Mai and Caroline, my daughter, for putting up with me as I hid away writing this book.

The likes of Billa and Christy Ring will never be repeated. Don't ask too much of God, just thank Him for what He gave us.

MICHAEL O'CONNOR

Early Days

I was born on Christmas day 1929. My mother died when I was six months old. My brothers and sisters and my Dad reared me. Annie Forde, from Greenmount, looked after us too. In my mind she is still part of the family. As I grow older fond memories come flooding back, as if life is now saying all those years are not gone and forgotten, they are a big part of me still.

All the magic and wonder of my childhood was woven around the Lough. It is where I belong. It is where all my thoughts and dreams and images first set sail for some distant shore. It was to me in summer time my peaceful Pacific Ocean, and in winter time my frozen North Pole.

In our childhood innocence, we drank from the Lough to quench our thirst in the summer evenings, exhausted from hurling on the green all day. Come the winter time, we would watch the ice creep along the crib-side first, around the bog, as we called it, where the rushes and trees are, where the swans and the ducks rear their young. When the church bell would ring at twenty to eight in the morning, out of bed I would jump, sensing this was the morning, down to John Anthony I would run, knowing the hour had come. Then across the wide part of the Lough we would crawl, slowly, step by step, inch by inch, with our hearts beating as we listened to every crack in the ice. When we reached the distant shore, over at Paddy Cantys, where the swings are now, we would jump and dance for joy. We were first across the ice. We had done it! Endless days of ice-skating had arrived, long before Euro-Sport was ever invented.

From that moment on there was only one rule, don't break the ice, and everyone observed that rule to the letter. The pure trust and sheer innocence around these events have given a permanent presence to them in my mind that still lives with me to this day.

Imagine our horror, when one day we saw members of the Lough Model Yacht Club, inside a paddle-boat, breaking the ice as they paddled along. I ran over crying to my Dad, shouting, 'Dad, Dad, they're breaking all the ice.'

Out he came, followed by my Uncle Paddy, who heard me bawling from next door. Over they went across the road and told the two gentlemen, in their paddle-boat, in no uncertain terms, to 'get out of that boat fast, stop breaking the ice. Ye have yer pleasure in summer, but the children have theirs in the winter.'

Out they got, boat and all, and that too has a permanent presence in my mind. I was so proud of my Dad that day, and still am to this day. He had kept the magic alive and restored to our young hearts the sheer delight of adventures yet to come. He understood that then, which is something I have never forgotten and never will.

Speaking of adventures yet to come, they came with Marshall Hudson. As the ice came, so did Marshall Hudson, like some tall migrant bird flying in for the season. He was a popular artist in the School of Art, a colourful character with a well-groomed beard. He wore a tweed hat and a long scarf thrown over his shoulder, and as he tied his skates he would repeat out loud, 'tell me now, who is first today, who is first today?'

We stood in line for a spin across the ice. I would hold on for dear life to the tail of his long tweed coat, as he swayed and circled on the frozen ice, with his arms outstretched and his head held high. I could feel the thrill and the speed of it, and the sound of my leather shoes, and the ice-cold breeze blowing in my face. He was carried away by his own performance, like a ballet dancer on stage in some other world, but all I wanted was to stay in this world, not to crash and sink and drown and never again see my Dad, or my brothers and sisters. I'm convinced Marshall Hudson gave me a love for family life, travelling at thirty miles an hour across the frozen Lough. My Dad had told me how the ice had broken once and a man slid under and drowned before rescue came. I, too, had fallen while skating on my own and still have the scar under my chin. Such thoughts as these sent terror through my mind, and made me grip the tail of the Marshall's coat with all the strength my little hands could muster.

It wasn't just in winter times these great adventures took place, and it wasn't all on ice. The day we borrowed the County Council boat, and set sail for Singapore had a wonder all its own. The County Council had the job of cleaning the Lough. They had a boat they used to moor on the crib-side, beside the wall, on a Saturday, and leave it there for the weekend. A few of my friends in our devil-ment decided we would borrow the County Council boat for a few hours. We untied the ropes and found no paddles. Home I ran, borrowed a sheet from my bed, and borrowed the sweeping brush from behind the kitchen door.

'Right lads,' I said, 'all hands on deck, put up that mast, and raise that big white sail.'

There was only one family of swans there in those dis-tant days, and they were used to us. They came around the crib-side too. They could see we were struggling to reach the open waters. They had their wings arched high above their backs, like the way the North Infirmary nuns used to wear their veils, and they sailed past us, making it all look so simple.

'Stop showing off,' I shouted.

Then a gust of wind caught the sheet. John Anthony held firm to the mast. We gathered speed, and away we sailed for Singapore, leaving the swans behind. 'That'll teach them a lesson,' I said, as we sailed into the sunset.

I can still see it all to this day, as I walk around the Lough with my wife. It still makes me happy to think about it. The Lough is, indeed, a sanctuary to me in more ways than one. It rested quietly then, with market gardens all around. It was a Cork of cobblestone, of trains trundling through streets, of trams and tracks, and bridges rising in the air. It had brewery horses, well-groomed and strong, knocking sparks out of stones as they marched along. Isn't it strange how memories can echo in your mind, bringing with it sadness as well as joy. To this day wherever I hear the clippedy-clop sound of a horse on the trot, I think of my mother. It was in a pony and trap she was taken that Christmas day back in 1929, to have her baby. No wonder my brother Teidy kept ball-hopping me as I was growing up, 'Willie boy, you're the Messiah the Jews are still waiting for.'

And what about my sisters, the day of the cloud-burst, when they ran out to bring in the clothes from the line? Who do you think had been outside, cloud-burst and all, only myself, standing in the tea-chest, all alone and forgotten, up to his ankles in water? Wasn't that some golden moment I had with Barry's tea! This was followed by an encounter I had with the big enamel bath, with those corrugated iron ridges around the sides, and me hanging on while I was scrubbed and rubbed, and dowsed like a dinky toy. Make no mistake about it, I have good reason to be cautious of water.

'We're proud out of you, Willie boy,' Teidy would say, by way of encouragement when he could see I was under pressure, and his next line then would be 'apart from the clothes you're wearing'. I used to get all his hand-me-downs, and one day he took a look at me and said, 'if you were to take off everything that's not yours, you'd be standing in front of me in your stocking vamps.'

You could say I grew up in a house where you had to be ready with a fast line to defend yourself. When it came to going to school, unfortunately, I wasn't in a position to defend myself from teachers' comments, but they were witty and I still remember them with great affection.

I went to Sullivan's Quay school down by the South Gate Bridge. I don't think the Christian Brothers or the teachers were ever anxious to boast about it, as myself and learning did not get on at all. God rest John O'Casey, an English teacher, who tried hard and used to say to me with no harm, 'Billa boy, you have a head, but so has a turnip.'

When it came to drawing, Brother Brigid, a low-sized man from Wexford, used to take one look at my artistic efforts and say, 'Billa, you couldn't draw your breath.'

Another day he brought me over to the windows. He was in a jovial mood. He pointed out the windows to the South Gate Bridge, where at the time all the idlers used to assemble. He started shaking his finger at the bridge. 'I want to tell you something boy, you are so thick, you won't even get a job sharing that bridge.'

It mustn't have been the South Gate Bridge at all he was pointing at – only Beamishs Brewery, where I spent thirty happy years.

I remember too when I was small, playing hurling night and day around the Lough, and many a time the ball went into the Lough. Then off would come my rubber dollies, and into the Lough I would wade, pulling up my short pants shorter. One day a woman sitting on the seat turned to me and said, 'little boy, that's too dangerous, wait for the tide to go out.' I'm still looking at her; and I still think of all the people who stroll around the Lough, and of the part it plays in the life of so many Corkonians. All the ducks and swans and wildlife, there in the heart of Cork's own beautiful city.

Many characters too have strolled around, what some people now call the cardiac circuit, for the good of their health. Raza springs to mind. He was a low-sized red-faced man, who always wore a peaked cap. His name was Jim Murphy, and he had a very sharp, but witty tongue. I can still remember the day I was playing in goal for Lough Rovers. After about ten minutes five or six goals were in behind me. Raza walks from the side-line, down to the edge of the square, and said, 'come off before the score is bigger than the attendance.'

Then to make matters worse, when an tAthair Liam Ó Reagáin said his first Sunday Mass in the Lough after he been transferred from Ballyphehane, he said in his sermon that he was at a dinner the night before in the Barrs Club, and he was sitting next to Gerald McCarthy. Gerald was talking about different people and games in the parish. You can imagine the shock I got sitting in the church, when he started talking about Raza and myself letting in all the goals. Fr Liam continued by saying I let in four goals. He told the story in a brilliant fashion and it was lovely to hear the loud laughter in the church. As I was walking out after Mass with my good wife, Nell, I met one of the ex-Lough Rovers players and I said to him, tongue in cheek, 'you know tAthair Ó Reagáin wronged me in there this morning with his four goals.'

'He wronged you all right Billa boy, I remember it well, 'twas seven goals.'

Isn't it terrible to have to put up with insults like that after Mass!

Another day around the Lough, I was walking Major, my loveable mongrel; and there was Raza sitting on a seat, basking in the sun, all on his own. Major went over by the seat. Raza turned to the dog and said, 'go home, ye mongrel.'

I put on my best Montenotte accent to upset Raza and said, 'let that animal be, I'll let you know, I have his papers.'

'If you have,' says Raza, 'they won't be stolen on ye.'

Raza worked in the Mills down on the docks and when John Power wrote that great play, all about dockers and hurling, Raza decided he would have to see it. It was called *As Some Tall Cliff* and James Stack produced it. I was playing the part of P. J., the son. It was a serious role. When I asked Raza what did he think of it, he gave me the supreme compliment, 'I hadn't time to light a fag with ye'.

Do you know what, if he was nice to me I'd get worried! He was a great Lough parish man, and would follow Lough Rovers to the ends of the earth. He didn't like defeat, but always took it fair and square. On one wet, miserable Sunday, Lough Rovers had been beaten badly. There in the silence of the dressing-room, after the match, a chap was packing away the jerseys into a gear bag. He turned to Raza and said, 'Raza, all the jerseys is runnin'.'

'They are the only things that ran today boy,' replied Raza.

Another day, close to Christmas, Raza went into Moks pub, and for poor Raza it was the morning after the night before. He was at the counter, barely able to hold up his pint. In comes this fellow with a harrier on a lead, and the dog kept prancing and dancing around the place, like Muhammad Ali in the ring. Raza turned, looked at the dog, and says, 'bite me, but for the love of God, don't bark.'

The poor man had a tragic death. He died, as a watchman down at the Mills, in a fire caused by an oil lamp – that was many years ago, but I have very fond memories of him, God rest him.

Another memory that hops in and out of my mind quite often is the day I spent as a young fellow in Clash in Little Island. It was the day my acting career began, and if it did not begin then, my instinct to survive got a kick-start. It happened in 1942 while Hitler had been on the rampage around Europe with tanks and guns and bullets flying, and we were around Cork on rations of brown bread and a half an ounce of tea per adult, per week. Maybe that's why my pals and I decided to go for a picnic, just to show Hitler he couldn't keep us indoors of a fine summer's day.

We set off early from the South Infirmary, walking down the Lower Road, Tivoli, passed the fields where the Silversprings hotel is now, on to the dirt roads to Clash in Little Island. Having spent a happy day playing around Clash in the woods and the open green fields, we decided to hit for home around 7.00p.m., tired and exhausted. Imagine the scene, six big weary twelve year old schoolboys, striking off for Cork through Glounthaune, with no cars on the road, so no chance of thumbing a lift.

A few lorries and traps passed us by but each in turn ignored the pleas of six scruffy schoolboys. I was under fierce pressure, thinking of the walk from Glounthaune to the Lough. Something had to be done. I slowed down and left my pals go well ahead of me by a couple of hundred yards. Then came music to my ears. I heard a pony and trap approaching and started immediately on my career in acting. I developed an awful limp. I dragged my right leg after me, without ever bothering to look at the people in the pony and trap. As they came up to me the man stopped the pony and trap and asked, 'how far are you going boy?'

I dragged myself up with my bad leg into the trap, doing the panting and the pale bit as well, and the wife of the driver was all concern.

'What is wrong with your leg, my darling little boy?' she asked.

Without batting an eyelid I replied, 'I got a bad fall a couple of weeks ago, mam.'

The best was yet to come. As I eventually passed my best friends, they roared, 'look at Billa, look at Billa!'

I just waved back at them, a slow dignified wave, better than the Queen of England ever did to her subjects. I was left off at Mangans clock in Patrick's Street and I limped away as the driver's wife wished me every blessing, hoping my leg would be better soon. For weeks after that I was terrified something would happen to my leg, as if God might do something to me; but God isn't like that at all.

Everybody in those days walked long distances and nobody believed they walked such distances. It was simply the done thing, and those who really wanted to travel got a bicycle. A Munster Final in Thurles would be a Saturday start for them; sleep in a Tipperary hay-stack, arrive mid-day Sunday; shout their heads off until five o'clock; start for home, win or lose, and be at your job at eight o'clock on Monday morning, no complaining.

My father walked me to many matches, often as far as Riverstown. The Magazine Road bus would go as far as The Cotton Ball and then we would walk the rest of the way to Riverstown. The likes of Douglas – where I first saw the Barrs win a minor title in 1938 – was no problem. I can still see our local jarvey, Johnny Cremin outside Douglas pitch and his horse proudly wearing the blue and gold ribbon of the Barrs on the bridle. I got a spin home from Johnny Cremin on his side-car, and how convenient it was, as Johnny kept his horse and side-car in the stables behind our house in the Lough. The way he used tell me to jump up as he would give me a lift was very uniquely Cork – 'Billa, cover the number, me old son.' This was a seat directly behind the jarvey, back to back with Johnny himself and his registered number was painted in a brass colour on that seat.

Many is the night I used to take Johnny's horse and put

away his side-car while he gave a demonstration of his days in the trenches during the Second World War. He would put a pike on his shoulder, and march up and down to the army drill. Then he would whistle as if calling a dog; and lo-and-behold, that horse would respond every night to his call of nature, before going to bed as it were.

The street leagues were like All-Ireland Finals in those days around the Lough. Danny Hobbs, that great Corkman and Barrs fan, was the founder member of the hurling street league in the Lough. I can still see Danny with hunting whip, cracking it loud and hard, to keep back the crowds, and my Uncle Paddy always assisted him.

I can still see the one famous final of a Sunday morning, with hundreds of people lined around the pitch at the Lough. Both teams had to march behind the Greenmount Band, all of them under eleven, and the ball was thrown in by none other than Jack Lynch himself.

I played many times in the street leagues, and we all got fourpence each. Our team, when paid, would head across the green over to O'Connell's shop, owned by my father, for the usual milk and odds (cakes).

We were all hurling heroes in our little hearts, and we all had the same burning desire to get to Croke Park to watch our heroes dressed in red. At the time there was talk all over the city and county about a young boy called Christy Ring.

However, I must say my route to Croke Park was very unusual, if not original, but I got there! It began with

Thompsons bakery where my father worked. They had bought a bog away up in North Cork, in Naad. My father told me that for every night I worked in the bog, stacking turf, it would be a railway station nearer to Croke Park. That was my wages. I set to work with great enthusiasm – Cork to Mallow one night; Mallow to Buttevant another night, and so on – until I made Croke Park to see my heroes, in 1944, achieve four in a row. What a game, but wait awhile! After the match, feeling great, with a Cork victory, we got a side-car from O'Connell Street to Kingsbridge Station, as it was then. I had a box of cream cakes and sand-wiches – that I guarded with my life for the train home – under my arm. As young as I was, I had a gut feeling the horse was going to fall as we drove down Ormond Quay, the way the man was treating the horse. I hung on for dear life to the rail, as my father, who sat next to me, and the two men on the opposite side, were advising the jarvey to take it easy on the horse, but to no avail. In the next few minutes down went the horse, the jarvey, my father and the two other passengers; but I still clung on to the rail, and with-out a scratch stepped on to the road.

There I was collecting my cakes and my sandwiches, and there was my poor father rubbing a lump on his head the size of an egg. As we walked away to head for the train, I had the misfortune to ask my father, 'did you have to pay the man, Dad?'

How is it he didn't lynch me, dump me or drown me in the Liffey, I'll never know, but a Cork victory had him in the best of humour and he only laughed, and the journey home was song and story.

My Days at Thompsons

I honestly believe I learned a tremendous amount about life in Cork during the happy days I spent in Thompsons. Out and about every day with a van full of cakes, listening to the people, to their joys and sorrows, their hopes and dreams. I felt I understood them and they understood me. I knew them in a way beyond their names, and many a time on stage that feeling would surface and lift my heart for the remainder of my performance. Applause at the end was like the audience saying, we understand you too, Billa. We know where you are coming from. That feeling has no price and no money on earth can purchase it.

Thompsons in McCurtain Street was a bakery like any bakery, or any other company in the city, with its own selection of characters, but obviously a few stood out more than the others. One such character was Maggie Butcher. She was a low-sized woman with glasses, and she worked in the bake-house; and at the time Thompsons had a very snobby Englishman in charge of the bake-house. He had that imperial tone. He would look at you, almost expecting you to bow down and genuflect.

He passed Maggie one day, and by his standards Maggie's overall wasn't up to scratch. As he passed her, he remarked with that English superior stiff upper lip, 'my God, the dirt of the Irish'.

'Excuse me boy,' says Maggie, 'our dirt can be cleaned,

but yer filth can't'.

'Come into my office,' he commanded, with the weight of the empire behind his voice.

'Get away,' says she, 'ye foxy eejit.'

That night the girls had a trade union meeting in the old Connolly Hall, next to St Patrick's church, and the next day our 'foxy eejit' had to apologise to Maggie. That was the day the British empire collapsed inside in my head, and in the heads of many others! That was the day I understood what James Connolly died for, and he did not die in vain.

You can appreciate how that Englishman did not have the same credibility after that. Then to add salt to the wound, another great character, Gerry Healy, poured boiling water so to speak on the poor man's wounded pride.

Our English friend had been listening to the Grand National in his car in Thompsons yard. Gerry Healy and myself were at the boot of his car, listening to the race as well. It was that famous and fateful day for Devon Lock, the queen's horse, who was only a few yards from the winning post. We could hear the English commentator having a stormer, 'a great day for Devon Lock, a great day for Her Majesty, a great day for England'.

We could hear our Englishman in the car cheering him on. Next we heard the wailing of the BBC commentator, 'he's down, he's down, he's down'.

'Come on,' says Gerry to me, going up to the car window, and in an innocent way asked, 'how's it goin' sir?'

The reply we got was a roar. 'Blast him and damn him.'

Gerry looked at him with innocent amazement written all over his face, and as roguish as ever, says in a very gentle voice, 'blast who sir?'

Our English friend shook his head, knowing he had been beaten twice, inhaled a deep breath and barked back, 'blast you, Healy, blast you.' Then he banged the door of his car and walked away. No wonder the English got out of Cork. The Rebel County showed no respect.

Thompsons, it could be said, was old Cork, before one-way streets, before traffic lights and traffic jams from motorcars. It had 'donkey's gudge' in big brown slices, with which you stuffed your face. It was Cork of barley sugar, liquorice allsorts, sticks of clove rock, white bon-bons and coloured marbles to play folly taw. Thompsons had stables full of horses and vans, and one winter's night Johnny Mahony was stuck with his horse and van in thick frost up in Evergreen Road. He phoned the wise man himself, Tommy Wilson, who used always say, 'a bad pencil is better than a good head'. Tommy was the foreman and he listened away to Johnny, all hot and bothered, stuck in the frost with his horse and van, complaining about the weather and the narrow streets up around Evergreen Road.

'I can't move, what am I going to do with the horse?'

'My advice to you is this, are you listening now, Johnny? Put yourself and your horse up in the nearest hotel,' the foreman said.

Johnny, to put it mildly, was not pleased and the foreman had a fair idea of the answer, so he dropped the phone as if it had been a hot iron. No wonder I had plenty of material, unscripted material, for *Up Cork* in the AOH Hall doing my Madgie Murphy every night, while I worked in Thompsons during the day.

Ignatius Comerford, that natural performer, my hero growing up, used play the star role in *Up Cork* and unfortunately he got a stroke in 1953 which ended his career in show business. I was asked to play Madgie Murphy and I'm glad to say *Up Cork* and myself went from strength to strength, seven nights a week, nine weeks being the shortest run, and one year it ran for sixteen weeks. Where did I get the energy I ask myself now on reflection? Being newly wed in 1955 I think had a lot to do with it. My best friend, my dear wife Nell, was a tower of strength. The support and companionship then and now is above and beyond what words can say. I was lucky in love. I'll leave it at that.

Replacing Ignatius Comerford was a big break for me now that I look back. But for me then, it was a young man full of imagination and drama, finally finding a stage to let out the energy. All my family had been involved in theatre as I grew up. My sister, Ann, played the Fairy Queen, and Teidy, my brother, played the Baron. Sheila, another sister, played the Fairy Queen in the AOH. So between Fr O'Leary Hall and the AOH, the O'Connell family were fully occupied year in year out with pantomime and variety shows of the day.

Those were the days before television, video, bingo and discotheques, and the city had many pantomimes in those days. Fr O'Leary Hall, AOH, Fr Mathew Hall, CCYMS, St Francis Hall. Coachford Town Hall was part of the scene too, and later on the panto arrived in Gurranabraher and the Glen Hall. The Opera House, of course, would have been the biggest stage of all, the dream come true, so to speak. The big names were Chris Sheehan, Chris Curran, Joe Lynch, Ignatius Comerford. I worked hard by day to make a living, and worked harder by night to try and make the crowd happy. Youth was on my side, and then when the pantomime season closed, along came the spring, and with it a festival called 'An Tóstal'.

We would be all asked to make the city look bright for An Tóstal; out would come the pots of paint, the brushes, window boxes and daffodils galore. This poor woman up in Blarney Street was painting away at her front door, when a neighbour asked her what was she doing.

'I'm getting ready for An Tóstal.'

'An what?' says the neighbour.

'An Tóstal,' replied the woman, annoyed to be asked a second time.

'May God give ye sense, after all your trouble he might not pass up this way at all.'

You can't win them all I suppose.

My experience in Thompsons went hand in glove with my stage career. One complemented the other. The accents I listened to every day were only highlighted on stage every night. I would lengthen the vowel on one word, and raise the tone on another. The reaction was great and the feeling on stage as a young man was wonderful. They were all my kind of people.

I used to do relief work when the van drivers would go on holidays, and this gave me many opportunities to meet more people. I used to spend a few days with the van driver, learning his route; and on one trip with this particular van driver, who was a very religious man, I happened to make a remark that upset him. We were driving out the Straight Road and the Lee Road was away over on my right across the river. My Auntie Lizzie, Mrs Kelly, lived in Mount Desert Lodge, right opposite Our Lady's grotto on the Lee Road. The religious van-driver pointed across the river saying, 'there she is, my lovely boy, she is a pal to us all.'

'That's right,' says I, 'she's an aunt of mine.'

Then it dawned on me, 'twas Our Lady he was talking about and not my Auntie Lizzie. No wonder I upset him,

Often my image on stage would spill over into my day job, and how often did it happen! When I would make a genuine mistake I'd be accused of 'can you take anything seriously', 'is there anything sacred with you?' Please allow for the possibility of my making a reply out of honest innocence, and not always with comedy in mind.

But I have to admit the Cork mentality thinks in witty terms almost permanently. Take for instance, this very small insignificant situation, yet the timing and turn of a word says it all. Jack Forde, one of Thompsons characters, went to ask a customer, Pearl McCarthy, who had a cake shop beside Sullivan's Quay school at the South Gate Bridge, for her Christmas order. She asked in return a very normal question, 'what size puddings do you have?'

'What do you think we have at Thompsons, a shoe factory?' Jack replied.

I have often thought about coming up with an answer to Jack from Pearl's point of view, and with no success. It again hit the nail on the head in relation to Cork humour, Cork city humour in particular. It is the reply that has no answer; and I often feel people outside Cork see us simply as 'smart asses' but what can we do! Hopefully the super-sensitive outside Cork appreciate where we are coming from, and if not, would they ever do a crash course on Corkology or Corkism, so that they could enjoy themselves far more; such is our way.

Every morning when Jack would come in to work he would have a debate going about sport or whatever he had heard in the news. During the war years, when Lord Haw-Haw was in his prime shouting propaganda against Britain, Jack came in one morning and said to Gerry Healy, 'were you listening to the radio last night? I tell you something, Haw-Haw gave it to John Bull, gave it hot and heavy', giving Gerry a verbatim account of what Haw-Haw had said.

As a ball-hop, as usual with Gerry, he replied, 'do you know Jack, I was listening to him as well, at home in Greenmount, and he didn't say anything like that at all.'

'Well if he didn't,' says Jack, in a most definite way, 'he

said it in Blackpool.'

To give you yet another example of what I mean I'll share with you a true story. I'm involved in a very small way with the Irish Guide Dogs, collecting boxes in different outlets. As you know these boxes are in many shops, supermarkets and pubs throughout the country, and a surprising amount of money is raised in this way. I had one box up in the coffee dock in the Bon Secour Hospital. Helen, the woman in charge, asked me to change boxes because the one I had given her was too big for the lip of the counter. I got her a small box, and I was transferring the money from the big box into the small box. A posh lady dressed in very fine clothes, with gold and silver dangling all over the place, was watching me closely and admiring what I was doing, saying, 'what a great cause the Guide Dogs are.'

I agreed with her.

'Do you know what,' she said, 'I think I'll make a contribution'. With that she took a pound coin out of her black leather purse and said innocently, 'tell me my good man, where is the dog's hole?'

Poor Helen nearly died with shock, when I turned to the woman and replied, ''tis where it's always mam, under his tail.'

In true Corkonian fashion, she burst out with laughter. The clothes she wore and the gold that shone so brightly round her neck, only added to the humour of the moment.

Here is another similar story, with a line that has no answer. I worked in Henry Fords for a short period in the body shop. I remember, during a very hot spell, going into work one morning for an eight o'clock start. The old dredger, going out the harbour, passed down the river, complete with buckets and smell. One of the lads on the dredger was slagging a pal of his going into Fords. 'Go on,' he shouted, 'go into your sweat box for the day, while I spend me day on the high seas.'

'High seas me eye,' replies my friend from Fords, 'you won't go past Blackrock Castle, and if you do go out further to dump your cargo, bring me back a monkey.'

The people who make these comments are wonderful people in my opinion. Even when it goes wrong I still enjoy the turn of phrase. I have to admit sometimes that an answer can backfire on you. A friend of mine, a great lover of dogs, was always walking his greyhounds. His daughter, a very attractive girl, was doing a line, as we say, 'with a fine catch'. The intended son-in-law called one night and my doggie friend opened the door for him.

'Is Tessie there?' he asked.

'She is sir,' replies my friend.

'By the way,' says the intended son-in-law, 'are you Tessie's father?'

'No sir, I only walks the dogs for the man of the house.'

Didn't he get five shillings for himself, and he had to take it. Wasn't it good enough for him?

My Days with Beamish & Crawford

When you retire from the company you have spent most of your life in, you begin to see it from a different point of view. While working, I felt part of a team, competing, promoting, selling and meeting targets. But when I walk past Beamishs now, it seems like a monument to many fond memories, and the brewery itself, standing there since 1792 is so much a part of Cork. I think of all the people that worked there, some from the same family, two and three generations, through troubled times and famine days.

How often did I rest my hand upon that stone on the entrance steps, and never gave it a thought. But now when I cast a cold eye upon it, I think of Morty Óg O'Sulllivan, who was an outlaw and a smuggler in the Beara Peninsula, and was killed in an attack on his hide-out in the 1750s. The story goes that this particular stone held the spiked head of Morty Óg. What a thing to do to any human being after you killed him! There is another stone over the fireplace in the boardroom, taken from an old pub on the site where the brewery is now, going back as far as 1602. In the boardroom itself there is a picture of Dr Love and Dr Webster, the Rector of Saint Nicholas, and the caption says 'The Flank Movement, doctors who don't differ' and there is Dr Love holding a bottle of old malt whiskey in his hand. Dr Webster's famous saying in the middle of the last century had been,

'The Temperance Movement of the present day is a flank movement of Christianity, led by the Devil.'

It is fair to say the name Beamish is very much part of Cork, providing work and a way of life for thousands of people since 1792. When that beautiful smell of hops and roast barley hangs in the air above the city, I feel at home. It reminds me of childhood at Sullie's Quay school, and when I return from a holiday in the sun, and get that very same smell, I know that all is well.

However, I must say, I had a very unusual start to my career with Beamish & Crawford. I wasn't all that long in the brewery, delighted with my new Cortina car, a big change from Thompsons van, when I called to a pub in Lismore. At that time, 35 years ago, you could let the car open and the keys in the ignition. I finished my call to the pub, sat into my car, as I thought, but I wasn't a minute behind the wheel when I realised I was in the wrong car. I got out, knocked at a door, asked the woman 'who owns the grey Cortina?'

'That's my husband's car,' she says.

I realised he had driven away the wrong car!

'You'll have a job to get him now,' says she, 'as he is a County Councillor for the area and he's gone to a council meeting in Dungarvan.'

Off I drove to get back my car. When I arrived at the County Council meeting, naturally a man in uniform refused to let me into the chambers.

'You can't go in there,' he said with authority, 'because there is a County Council meeting in progress.'

'If there is,' says I, 'there is one chipalata of a councillor in there that doesn't know his arse from his elbow, because he took my car, and drove it from Lismore to Dungarvan'.

In he went like a shot, brought out my councillor and when he saw who he had he said, 'Billa, is it the Freedom of Dungarvan you want?'

'No,' says I, 'all I want is the keys of my car.'

Wasn't that a nice start to my new flashy job, but I enjoyed it immensely. I have happy memories. It suited my temperament. Where in all the world would you hear a story like this, and be getting paid while listening?

I used to call once a week to a very illustrious bar in Patrick's Street, the Chateau. One day I went in and standing at the counter was Tom Donnelly, manager of the Opera House at the time, and Pat Murray, artistic director. Joan Denise Moriarty, that wonderful lady of ballet, was with them.

The Ballet Company were opening that night in the Opera House. They asked me to join them for a coffee, and in the course of the conversation Joan Denise said, 'Billa, I hope you'll come to support the ballet this week.'

'Well, Miss Moriarty,' says I, 'my wife and daughter always go to see the ballet, but to tell you the truth, I don't understand too much about it.'

'Well, Billa,' says she, 'I always go and support your shows, and I certainly don't understand you.'

No wonder I enjoyed my job.

Another day below in Mossy Reaney's pub in White-gate, the one straight across from the Oil Refinery, I was having a bowl of soup and a sandwich with the local lads. In came two blokes with Dublin accents and asked me innocently, 'what are all the tanks across there?'

I turned and said to the delight of the locals, 'that's our local creamery.'

Another publican I used to call to near Shandon took great pride in keeping his pub in the old fashioned style – a big roaring fire and flagstones for a floor. A lot of Americans called into him during the holiday season. One day an American arrived, complete with camera, gold tooth and big belly and ordered a glass of the local brew. He got his glass of stout, started to smoke a cigar as big as the glass, and eventually turned to the publican and said, 'I say, have you got an ashtray?'

The publican looked at him straight in the eye and said, 'my good man, you're standing on it.'

Another pub I had the pleasure of calling to was Clancys, Princes Street, on behalf of Beamishs for fifteen years. Gerry O'Sullivan, God rest him, his wife, Margaret and their son, Dan became personal friends rather than customers. Gerry asked me would I do a turn at Dan's wedding in Innishannon House. I normally don't do this type of show but I couldn't refuse a great friend. Dan married a Cork city girl, but the majority of Gerry and Margaret's family and friends were natives of Ballingeary and Inchigeela. Down I went to

Innishannon House, entertained the guests, complete with dress, wig and handbag, and as we say in the theatre world, thank God, I had a blinder. Gerry went down the following weekend to his relations and friends in Ballingeary, and one old grandaunt told Gerry, "twas one great day, Gerry, but didn't the one from the other side leave them down very badly.'

God rest poor Gerry, I can still hear him laughing when he told me this.

I always feel genuinely sorry for people who say they are bored with their job, hate going to work and wish they could retire in the morning. I'm not too sure it is related to lack of money, lack of status or no future in what they are doing, from their point of view. I have always put great faith and trust in a good colleague, although on a few occasions I have tested that faith to the limit.

Joe Nolan, a very warm-hearted man, was always involved in some ball-hop or other in the brewery, especially with the sales reps. As he came in one morning to the office he said, rather fussed, 'I'm kind of late.'.

'What a morning you're late,' says I, 'Tony Halpin is looking for you.' Tony Halpin was our managing director.

Joe gave his hair a bit of a comb, the shoes a bit of a rub, and off with him down to Tony Halpin's office where there was a board meeting in progress.

'Well Joe,' said Tony Halpin, 'can I help you?'

Joe put me out to dry straight away when he said, 'Mr

Halpin, Billa O'Connell told me you're looking for me.'

'Joe, do you realise the day you have, April the 1st. I'm afraid you have been had,' said Tony to the sound of chuckles all round.

When Joe arrived back to the sales reps office, I was half way between Cork and Fermoy on my journey!

Another evening I was in the Commodore Hotel, Cobh, owned by the O'Shea family. A big function was taking place that night, and the Carling taps weren't pouring properly. I knew there was somebody in the brewery service department who would help me and fix the taps but as 'twas gone five o'clock, I also knew our telephone would be manned by John Pat Duggan. After five o'clock there was no way past John Pat. He was on strict instructions not to allow any calls into the brewery after five o'clock.

Here I was in the Commodore Hotel, no Carling pouring and there and then I got a brain wave. I was able to imitate Mr Beamish, with his husky voice. I often did it in his presence, to his delight. I phoned John Pat, letting on I was Richard Beamish. All I said was, 'hello John Pat, Beamish here.'

He nearly came through the phone to me, with the excitement of the boss phoning. 'Can I help you sir?'

'Put me on straight away to the service department.'

The job was done, the taps were fixed, the Carling flowed and everybody happy.

As I said, we all need colleagues, in whom we can place our trust. To hold on to a sense of humour is important if you want to avoid stress in the workplace. I remember one morning going up to the sales reps office, which is at the top of a very steep stairs. Donal Kenneally, our promotions manager at the time, was going up the stairs with me. It was around nine o'clock in the morning and there was an electrician working away, changing a fluorescent light. It went dark suddenly. Donal whispered to me, 'fall William, fall down.'

I stumbled back a few steps, left an almighty roar, dropped my order book, and said, 'Oh God, I'm dead'.

'Come here Mac, did you see that?' said Donal to the electrician.

Straight away he went on the defensive, stared at Donal Kenneally and said, 'I saw nothing, okay, I saw nothing.'

Donal replied as fast as lightning, 'if there was a few thousand in it for you, you'd see it.'

Comments such as these give a life and vibrancy to the ordinary routines of every working day. I was always on the lookout for them and once I would hear them, I would remember them forever. They became like secrets in my head, but a secret is not really a secret until you tell somebody, and maybe the time has come now to divulge the boldest two secrets I have kept for a long time. I call it my Johnny Cash secret and my secret with the law.

Beamishs booked Johnny Cash for the *Cork 800* show in the Opera House and all five performances were sold out. During the weekend Johnny Cash wasn't feeling well and a doctor had to be called. He spent a lot of time in his dressing-room between performances. Naturally, Beamishs had a lot of publicans invited to the shows over the weekend. I remember Noel Howell, who was the sales director at Beamishs, brought back about twenty programmes to be autographed by Johnny Cash for the publicans. Knowing that Johnny Cash was resting in his room, not feeling well, I had not the heart to torment the man, so I got a biro and in my best theatrical scribble I wrote on every single programme, *Best Wishes, Johnny Cash*. Noel Howell was ever-grateful saying, 'only you could have done it boy.'

My secret with the law happened on a Christmas week, and I driving through East Cork, not thinking of speed traps. A squad car stopped me. I couldn't pull up as I had a full keg of Carling in the back seat for a customer. I eventually backed back to the guard, rolled down the window, and the first greeting I got was, 'well, it had to be you'.

I then genuinely and sincerely apologised to him for not stopping, because if I had I would have gone through the window, keg and all.

'I'll accept that,' says the guard, 'but what is your excuse for doing 50 mph in a 30 mph zone?'

'To tell you the God's truth guard, Christmas week I'm up the walls, I must have been day-dreaming.'

'That's true, Christmas times, go on away and slow down like a good boy.'

I thanked the guard again and explained if he had fined me, it would be nothing out of my pocket because the brewery would pay the fine. 'So now guard, let me thank you for your kindness, I have a few six-packs in the boot, I won't see you short for Christmas,' I said.

'My lovely boy,' says he, 'do you want me to lose my job and pension, taking drinks from you in a public road.'

'I'll solve that for you. Tell me where you're living,' says I, taking out my little black book I used to have for brewery business.

'Well,' says he, 'in all my years in the force, Billa, you're the greatest cowboy I ever met. You are the first man I ever stopped to summons and end up being asked for my name and address.'

Hadn't I the cheek – but we were the best of friends ever after.

Now that I have risked two secrets I'll risk one more; but it is in a confessional box I should be telling this one, not in a book for publication. Richard Beamish, the very man himself with the very famous name is central to this tale with a moral slant. He was a low-sized dapper man, elegantly dressed. He used to wear a pink silk handkerchief flowing from his top pocket to match the pink carnation on his coat. He was indeed one of Cork's own merchant princes, and proud we were of him, but he did have a short fuse and often spoke in divers tongue.

One day before Christmas he called me into his office, sat me down and said, 'Billa, I have been stopped by a guard, by the old *Inisfallen* berth, down at Horgan's wharf. I must admit, I lost the cool, Billa, do the best you can.'

I proceeded knowing the task ahead would not be easy,

but the minute the guard saw me getting out of the car, he told me not to waste his time, that Mr Beamish had verbally blown him out of the river. I was cornered, stuck for words, and as a last resort, despite the coming season of Christmas and all that entails for a struggling Christian, I decided to risk a white lie. 'You'll see this Christmas, guard, and many Christmases to come; but poor old Dickie Beamish, God love him, will be lucky to see Easter, and if you were in his position, you would be cranky too.'

I must have touched a chord in his heart, because straight away he showed compassion for Mr Beamish. When I got back to the brewery Mr Beamish asked me how I got on. I told him the job was sound, and I couldn't get out of his office fast enough in case he asked me what I said to the guard.

Mr Beamish lived for many years after, and at regular intervals, anytime I met the guard, he would shout out with laughter, 'Billa, you are some bloody liar, that man is healthier than myself.'

But how could you refuse the man who gave the world that soft dark drink with the lovely aftertaste. He was a man of class. His presence in company was electric and the place would come alive. He had the style and grandeur of Savile Row, with the hanky flowing down every day to his navel; but he was a man of sound humanity, a wonderful character.

When Seán Lemass, the Taoiseach at the time, opened Beamishs new bottling plant back in the 1960s, all the publicans were invited for the occasion, and later on all retired to the hospitality tent. Late into the evening a certain publican came up to Mr Beamish and said, 'I have had a great day here today, and I would like to buy you a drink out of here by way of thanking you.'

Being the great diplomat that he was, Mr Beamish replied, 'of course, let's go across the road.'

On his way out with the publican he passed me and commanded, 'Billa, follow me.'

Off I went like a terrier on a scent, following the publican and Mr Beamish. The minute we entered the pub Mr Beamish said to the owner, 'drinks for the house'.

Pints of Beamish flowed like buttermilk. Over in the corner was this poor misfortune, God-help-us kind of character sitting on his own. A pint of Beamish was put in front of him, and he thought Christmas had come early.

'Who's that from?' he asked.

'That's a pint of Beamish, from Mr Beamish.'

Up he got, with his pint in his hand, and made his way towards Mr Beamish, saying, ''tis a pleasure to meet you sir. Here's to your health, and I wish you the very best, the very very best.'

Then he stopped suddenly, as if taken aback, looked down at the pink hanky, and up at Mr Beamish, down again at the hanky, and up again at Mr Beamish. Out he stretches his hand, and with his big finger, bate the silk hanky back into Mr Beamish's top pocket, saying in a very corrective way, 'excuse me sir, but your hanky is all sticking out' and back he went to his corner, all alone once more. Mr Beamish was indeed a gentleman that evening. He threw a glance in my direction, smiled, closed his eyes for a second or two, and never ever mentioned the incident to me or anyone else ever after. He was indeed a man of substance, a quality I believe not linked to wealth or power or fame. I admired him as a man, regardless of position.

He was a great man for the horses and had no knowledge of any other sport. He had been a steward for the Turf Club of Ireland. Carling sponsors the Tralee races every year, and there's always a marquee to entertain guests. Tralee Races are held in September, and the Kerry football team who were to play in the All-Ireland Final were invited as guests. Being a GAA man myself, I got the job of greeting the team on arrival, and also because I knew Niall Sheehy through concerts I had done for his father, the famous John Joe Sheehy. As Niall was captain I introduced him to Mr Beamish, and Niall in turn introduced Mr Beamish to the players. When the introductions were over, the first question Mr Beamish asked Niall Sheehy was, 'and tell me,' he says, 'where's the final being played this year?'

When Mr Beamish eventually moved away, Niall said to me, 'Billa, where did you get your man, and did he ever hear of Croke Park, and does he not know the final is played there every year?'

'Don't be so smart,' says I, 'wasn't it played in the Polo Grounds in New York in 1947.'

I love Kerry but I couldn't let down my own crowd!

Raymond O'Rahilly, of Beamish & Crawfords, was a good hurler for Sars, and is a good golfer at this present time. His wife, Kay, my wife Nell, and myself meet regularly and many years ago the four of us went to the Canaries and one day we went on a trip to Puerto Rico. As we were making our way home, we passed a private villa and for the first time in our lives we saw lemons growing on a tree. Nell took out her camera, saying, 'I must take a photo of these lemons to show the children when we get home.'

Just inside the railings of the villa there was a big heavy man, sunning himself and relaxing, and sipping brandy, and at the same time he seemed to be studying a financial paper about stocks and shares. He got very annoyed when he saw Nell taking a photo of his lemons and I'm sure he was telling her what to do with her camera in his native Spanish tongue. As we were on the public thoroughfare we simply ignored him and Nell kept taking her photos. Raymond was greatly amused by the whole thing; had your man well studied with his brandy and big belly and studying the stocks and shares. Ray said in his own simple and innocent way, 'excuse me sir, I see you're reading the paper there, could you tell me is there any news of the Fair Hill drag hunt?'

As we were doubled up laughing at Raymond's comment, your man threw his eyes to heaven, and stormed back into his villa.

CORK LOCAL WIT

I have always adored listening to the people of Cork, the man on the street as they say. The comic timing I often heard outside Roches Stores in Patrick Street would beat many an artist strutting his stuff on stage. The most pleasant aspect of these chance meetings is that they don't see themselves as funny, they don't set out to be humorous at all. It is just a very unique part of what we are.

Sometimes people outside Cork get the wrong impression, and think we can be saucy, bordering on the arrogant, but I can assure them, the reverse is closer to the truth. We don't like outsiders trying to be clever in a subtle way, trying to put us down and make us feel silly and us Corkonians deliver an answer that clearly says, 'we can smell your subtle put-down a mile away'.

To give an example of this, let me take you down the Lower Road, to the start of the dual carriageway, just beyond Silversprings Hotel, where to this day the figure of a big dog in stone lies over the front of a gate. Two Americans were taking photographs of the dog one day, when a local wit passed along, out on his daily stroll. The Yanks, trying to be witty and very clever, said, 'excuse me Paddy, how often do they feed that dog?'

Without breaking his stride, he turned to the Yanks and said, 'whenever he barks'.

I think I have made my point. You see us Corkonians

have no problem with the real scholar. People of learning we know to be truly humble of heart. They are admired, that is why we like to upstage those who have notions about their intelligence – Cork humour has a very sharp edge.

An Englishman, with an air of brashness about him, was passing Fr Mathew statue one day, and he asked a Cork wit, 'who is that man on the statue?'

'That's Fr Mathew, sir,' came the reply, 'the apostle of temperance.'

'But why is he holding his hand out straight?' asked the Englishman with a smirk.

'He's telling the people of Cork, they're drinking since they're that height.'

Need I explain any further!

Cork wit is best found in the answer. It is in the reply, to which there is no further reply.

Jack Cowhie had a plumber's shop in Tuckey Street and did a lot of contract work for Beamishs. I can still see Jack to this day, with a bag of tools on one shoulder and a ball-cock on the other.

One of our managers, from Canadian Breweries at the time, sent for Jack one morning to tell him that his wife had lost her gold watch down the toilet in their house in Lovers-walk, in Montenotte, and would he kindly try and retrieve it.

Up Jack went with his helper, and after two hours of pushing and shoving with brushes and plungers, the lady in question put her head out the window and said, 'Mr Plumber, did you find my watch yet?'

Quick as a flash Jack replied, 'Mam, there's so much shit out here, you couldn't find Shandon.'

A Cork worker made redundant and thought he'd never see a bad day again. He got a stack of money and signed on once a week in the Exchange. One day when he returned from the Exchange his wife says to him, 'what ails ye, what's wrong with ye, you look very drawn and pale?'

'I'm just after coming out of the Exchange, and they are after offering me a job.'

'Oh Lord,' says she, 'and we just getting on our feet.'

When Dinny Allen, Cork sportsman, got engaged to Frances Barry-Murphy, sister to Cork's own legend, Jimmy Barry-Murphy, they arrived into Nemo Rangers Club, where there was great excitement and celebrations. Joe Joe Donnelly, a well-known Cork bookie and great dog man, asked what was all the excitement about. He was told Dinny Allen had got engaged to Frances Barry-Murphy.

'Do you know what,' he says, 'I'd give two thousand pounds for the first pup.'

Dinny Allen, he could give a reply, no better boy. I was at a match one summer's evening out in Nemo Rangers pitch when a row started between the players. Dinny ran on to the pitch to calm things down. On his way back to the side-line, a fellow from the opposition shouted from the bank, 'I bet you'll have that in your *Echo* column on Saturday night Dinny.'

'I will, boy, but you won't be able to read it.'

The crowd erupted.

I met some great characters in Cobh in my travels as a rep for Beamishs. One such character was Sharkey, who worked in the Cunard line. He served in the USA army and was very proud of the fact that when President Eisenhower passed through Cobh, he had his photograph taken with Sharkey.

One day I saw Sharkey outside the Commodore Hotel checking his betting dockets against the *Evening Echo*. I saw him tearing up the dockets, none too pleased.

'Did they come in for ye Sharkey?' says I.

'They did,' says he, 'if I backed the tide 'twouldn't come in.'

I remember doing a tour with Michael O'Duffy, a famous tenor at the time. Our pianist was Norman Metcalfe, and we also had Tadhg O'Leary, a well-known Cork baritone with us; and over the weeks Tadhg and Norman became great friends.

Our last night had been in the town hall in Mallow and Norman Metcalf was staying in the Central Hotel in Mallow. He asked us back for an end-of-tour, traditional, farewell drink. The dawn itself was breaking before we said our final farewells. We were walking down the street, a little way from the hotel, when Norman's voice rang out from his hotel bedroom window saying, 'go home ye parcel of Cork drunken whores.'

'My good friend Norman, you're a poor judge of women,' Tadhg replied.

You see Cork humour puts you in your place, the answer is the key. It is our inoffensive way of saying as politely as we can 'who the hell do you think you are?'

A neighbour of mine used always be very annoyed and upset when she saw people walking their dogs around the Lough, messing and soiling the pavements. One day she confronted this man with his dog, saying, 'I'm going straight to the City Hall, to complain about your dog destroying the Lough every day.'

'You're right too Mam, off you go, and when you're down there, don't forget to complain about the swans and the ducks and seagulls doing the very same.'

A great friend of the family was Dr Jim Young, of Cork and Glen Rovers fame. He was our family doctor for many years and a great friend of ours and always paid a visit when in the area. My son, Bill, was only a few months old when he got sick on a Sunday morning of the County Final between the Barrs and the Glen. I didn't fancy ringing on the day that was in it, but my family came first. I phoned and up he came in a few minutes. I can still see the scene. There was Bill, a few months old, lying in his cot with a knitted blue cardigan on him. When the doctor saw him he looked at the cardigan with a twinkle in his eye. 'Before I look at the child, take that thing off him.'

Once when Dr Jim was doing locum and helping out a fellow doctor he got a call to go out around the Bishopstown area to visit a Mrs Murphy who was expecting a baby at the time. It was dark. Dr Jim got lost. He knocked on this door for directions, asked the lady did she know of a Mrs Murphy in the neighbourhood, 'and to help you,' says Dr Jim, 'I can tell you she's pregnant.'

The woman was annoyed at being called to the door and in a sarcastic voice she said, 'I know of no Mrs Murphy living around here pregnant.'

'I tell you,' says Dr Jim, 'if she was single you'd know of her.'

Many years ago when the Barrs bought Páirc Uí Neanáin in Togher, they organised a finance committee to raise money to pay off the debt. One of the ventures arranged was a pantomime in Fr O'Leary Hall. It ran for many weeks and was a huge success – we were sold out days in advance. Tony O'Shaughnessy, Barrs and Cork hurler, was Chairman of the Finance Committee. During the pantomime, the Barrs and Lough Rovers met in the final of the McCurtain Cup, a junior hurling competition. Tony Shaughnessy was playing full-back for the Barrs and the final was fixed for a Sunday morning in the old Athletic Grounds. That very Sunday we had a matinee at 3.00 p.m. and a night show at 8.00 p.m. During the course of the game, I was brought on as a sub as left-corner forward for Lough Rovers. The first ball broke down by the corner-flag and I ran out to collect it, followed by the Barrs right-full back. Tony Shaughnessy's voice rang out, thinking of the successful pantomime and the money pouring in for the Barrs, and he shouted, 'don't touch him, don't touch him!'

Fr Nessan was a Capuchin, well-known and well-loved by all Corkonians. He spent many years in Rochestown, Holy Trinity and his last years in Gurranabraher. He was a great lover of sport of all kinds. I went to his funeral Mass in Gurranabraher and the priest who gave the homily spoke highly of Fr Nessan – about how much he was loved by his people and how much he loved his people.

He told the story of Fr Nessan walking up the hills of Gurranabraher and meeting one of his parishioners, a young married woman, with one child in her pram, one holding on to the left side and another holding on to the right side. He looked sympathetically at the woman, and said fondly to her, 'have you far to go, my good woman?'

And her simple reply was, 'October, Father.'

Leonard Barry, a loveable character, lived on Bandon Road, a few doors away from Moks pub. Everybody knew him as Big Barr because he was a very big man in every way. His father, Mr Barry, used play the cello in the Opera House. I can still recall Mr Barry to this day and he always wore the wagtail coat. Every Saturday night Big Barr had to go to the

Opera House and swag the cello up to Fair's Cross. He was in Fair's Cross one evening with perspiration dripping off him and as he leaned on the cello he said to the lads at the cross, 'Larry Adler made millions out of playing a mouth-organ, the size of a sausage, and my ould fellow had to pick the bull fiddle.'

I used to meet Big Barr every morning in Dinny Crowley's shop when I was delivering cakes for Thompsons. One morning when the shop was crowded with customers, including Big Barr and myself, a woman ran in crying her eyes out. 'Mr Barry, Mr Barry,' she says, 'my dog is missing, and I wouldn't mind, but the last time he went missing the overcoat I knitted for him was stolen.'

Big Barr looked at her and said, 'an overcoat, I can tell you something girl, he has more than what I have.'

Big Barr convinced me that morning that humour is a great cure for stress, because she calmed down in an instant.

Another great Cork character was Paul O'Donovan, a rep for Murphy's Brewery. In the soccer world he was known as the Golden Boy, God rest his soul. 'Tis only a fool would take on the golden boy.

One day he went into the pub in Shandon Street which was packed with customers and a smart alec took Paul on straight away by saying, 'here Paul, the Guinness traveller is just gone out the door, and he called for the house.'

'Oh Lord,' says Paul, 'and I missed him again.'

Before Murphy's had been taken over successfully by Heineken the Murphy reps were selling everything, spirits, bottled beers, minerals, etc. This day Paul had a whiz-kid out from the marketing department promoting Canada Dry. They called to Aggies at the top of Blarney Street and the marketing man asked the gentleman at the bar-counter, 'tell me, my good man,' he said, 'would you drink Canada Dry?'

''Ere sir, to tell you the truth I'd drink Europe dry.'

I called to the Swan and Cygnet in Patrick's Street one day during the holy hour, between 2.30–3.30 p.m., when the pubs were supposed to be closed, and 'twas packed to the doors. While I was talking to Jim Clancy and getting my order, the pub was raided. In came two guards who started taking names straight away. I knew I had no problem because one of the guards knew I was from the brewery, when he saw my order book and briefcase. While they were taking down the names, up came a real small mickey dazzler of a fellow and said, 'Billa, when the guard comes around, I'll tell him I'm working with you in the brewery.'

'No trouble, have a go if you wish.'

The guard came up and asked your man for his name. Straight away the answer the guard got was, 'I'm working with Billa in the brewery.'

The guard had one look at him and the way he was dressed. 'Are you off your head?' says the guard, 'if you're working in the brewery I'm the King of Siam.'

Another Cork character, a man I knew well, was Slobby Malone. I mentioned him one time on the *Late Late Show* and of course all the wise men in all the pubs kept on telling Slobby that he should catch Billa and Beamishs for thousands. He called a few times to the brewery but never got past security.

One summer's evening, as I passed by the Trinity church, there was Slobby having a snooze up against the railings. I tiptoed as quietly as possible past him but all in vain. Just as I passed, a voice rang out, 'Billa, you owe me thousands, although right now I'll settle for the price of a quart', which I promptly gave him. We shook hands and parted good friends.

I remember, in my teens, a loveable character from the northside, called the Rancher, who went up for the local elections. His real name was McCarthy. Klondyke, also known as Dr Healy, was in the same campaign. Klondyke's slogan was, 'Get me in and I'll get ye a ladies toilet'.

The Rancher's reply was, 'Put me in, and ye can go anywhere'.

One morning, when I was working in Thompsons, I was asked to deliver cakes in Church Street. Next to the shop I noticed the Rancher's box-car, an ordinary timber box-car, with the round ball-bearing wheels, and he had his election slogan on the side of his box-car, 'Burn the Rancher's blocks, vote McCarthy No 1'.

Next I heard ructions in the hall near the shop. The

Rancher came into the street after a loud argument with his wife. Seeing a strange young fellow delivering cakes, he was a bit embarrassed having had a row with his wife during an election campaign, 'do ye hear her, won't she make a lovely Lady Mayoress.'

There's confidence for you!

I have been in and out of the Bons a few times, thank God with nothing serious. I remember I finished a pantomime on a Saturday night, and had to be in the Bons on Sunday, to be operated on Monday for gallstones, which had given me a lot of trouble during the pantomime. As I was being wheeled down the corridor, half knocked out, I remember the nurse who was wheeling me, put her hand into my mouth saying, 'Billa, I forgot to take out your teeth.'

A battle started there and then, and I trying to tell her in my dazed condition, 'my teeth are my own!'

When I arrived into the operating theatre, there was Mr Kiely, that very kind and nice man. I heard him say to the staff, 'here's Dame Dollie from the panto, we'll keep her quiet for a while!'

A great friend of mine was the late Sister Agatha of the Bons hospital. A larger than life character, she worked around the Lough parish calling to various houses, looking after the sick. Her assistant was Sister Dominica, still hale and hearty in the Bons. I got to know Agatha well because my wife's mother stayed with us when she wasn't well, and Agatha was a regular visitor.

One day coming up the South Main Street, Sister Agatha was standing by the bus stop. I duly opened the passenger door and in she got. When she sat into the car with a sigh of relief she said, 'may God bless you, I'm standing at that bus stop for the last hour and a half, and me arse is like concrete.'

I have lovely memories of St Finbarr's Hospital – the reason being that after all our shows in AOH Hall, be it pantomime or *Up Cork,* it was always on our calendar to bring the show to the hospital. It was a small little hall with a lovely stage, and the main attraction for me was the supper we all got from the nuns afterwards.

This particular night we were getting dressed backstage and as there were no dressing-rooms we got ready in one of the male wards. I was about to take off my shoes and sat on a bed, which I thought was empty, when I heard a roar, a cough, and a grunt. Up I hopped straight away, to find a man in the bed, so thin he was like a wrinkle under the bedclothes. He looked at me from under the sheet and said, 'come here boy, are you trying to kill me before me time?'

My lovely memory of that same night was when Fr Feeley, who was chaplain at the time, gave a bottle of whiskey and a few cases of pint bottles to the cast. In fairness the cast had one look around the ward, called the nurse, asked for a few empty glasses and gave the whiskey and the pint bottles out to the patients.

While the show was going on downstairs little did the nuns and staff know that a better party was going on upstairs. I can still recall, as we were leaving to go over to the convent for supper, my wrinkle who was out of the bed with a big long night-dress down to his ankles, a pint bottle in his hand, and he singing for us all, cast, nurses and patients, 'The Valley of Slievenamon'.

Paddy Cotter used to tell a lovely story about the time he was working in Lee Boot. Cork United got into a cup final and a bus outing to Dublin was arranged. They left the Opera House at 8.00 a.m. and the bus apparently was a bit of a banger. Coughing, spluttering and backfiring, it never went over 10 mph. As they were going down the Lower Road to Dublin, a wit shouted from the back of the bus to the driver, 'come here Mac, is there an engine in this or are you only pedalling?'

A story credited to Chris Sheehan is about the late Dr Daniel Coughlan, Bishop of Cork, lovingly known as 'Danny Boy'. As he got on in years he was going towards the cathedral one day when a parishioner stood in front of him and he said, 'who have I here?'

"Tis Hannah Murphy, me Lordship.'

'And tell me Hannah, what is the problem?'

"Tis the daughter me Lordship, she's in the family way.'

With a twinkle in his eyes he said, ''Ere Hannah my girl, when she'll be my age, she'll be in everybody's way.'

A neighbour of mine who lived out by the Lough was Danno Crowley. We grew up together as he lived in Bandon Road before he got married. He was a very heavy man, but very witty. I met him one day around the Lough and he says, 'I'm listening to fellows there boasting about doing ten rounds, twelve rounds, fifteen rounds of the Lough a day.'

In my own innocent way I said, 'how many would you do yourself, Dan?'

He turned to me and says, 'I do four a day – four seats.'

Where Sevilles' shop in Oliver Plunkett Street is now, there used to be a cinema called the Imperial. It was known locally in Cork as Miahs, and anytime I would come home and be asked what picture house I went to, I always told a white lie because I would be in deep trouble if I said I was in Miahs.

One Saturday afternoon in the middle of a cowboy picture, with Indians and arrows all around the place, the projector broke down. The whole cinema was left in darkness. A voice shouted 'what's the problem?'

A Cork wit replied, 'Miah must be after falling off the butter-box.'

The same kind of humour was over in the Assembly Rooms in the South Mall, lovingly known as The Assembs. The man in charge of the tickets was a low-sized man called Georgie. Any time there was someone shot in the film, the cry went up, 'Georgie, take out the body'.

Jackie Sullivan, a great hurler of the 1940s, lived in Lough Road and he a tall man with a sharp tongue. I can recall during Lent there was a mission in all churches all over the city, and people would be comparing missions in the different churches. The first week was for the women and the second week for the men. I was working in Fords during the day and doing shows at night and I used always miss the Sunday night opening of the mission. The shift I had in Fords was 6.00 a.m. to 2.30 p.m., not a nice shift on a winter's morning. I used to call to Jackie Sul in his house on the Lough Road around 5.30 a.m. to head off down the Marina to Fords. As Jackie had been at the mission the night beforehand my first question was, 'what kind was the missioner last night?'

'What kind was he?' says Jackie. 'He said everything bar mention my name.'

Those were the days of fire and brimstone.

Another memory of Jackie Sul was when we were going around by the South Gate Bridge at the bottom of Barrack Street at 5.30 a.m., and I had my lunch under my arm. Being a growing boy, 'twas so big it was more like a horse's feed bag. There were three guards standing at the bottom of Barrack Street hill. Jackie and I said, 'good morning guards'.

One of the guards, thinking he was a wit, looked at the size of my lunch and said, 'are ye going on a picnic?'

Sullie answered him, thinking about where he was going for the next eight hours, panel beating in Fords of a winter's morning. 'Guard,' says he, "tis a quare picnic.' Then he whispered to me, 'they don't have a clue Billa, me with me hammer on one hand and my little anvil on the other, tap, tap, tap on the cold sheet metal hour after hour.'

'Not a clue Sul boy, but we'll soldier on' was the only answer I could think of that hour of the morning.

Pa Dunne was an insurance agent and he tells a story about a fellow who ran into him with a motor-car. The motorist got out and said to Pa, 'you gave me no signal.'

Pa looked down, saw his indicator flicking away and said, 'here, what do you think that is – Roches Point?'

For years I was entertainment's manager in the Country Club. I know that's a grand title for me! All I was doing was booking the bands for every Saturday night. Helping us out at the door was my brother-in-law, Donie O'Brien, who worked in the fire brigade, a loyal friend and a very witty fellow.

This particular wet and stormy Saturday night we had a very poor house. As I stood with Donie and Pearse Moore, the proprietor, along came the owner of a flea-ridden mangy dog, who approached the door hoping to get in out of the weather. Donie turned to us and said, 'if he comes another foot I'll charge him.'

Just inside the door of the Country Club was the cigarette machine. One night the machine wasn't working properly and coins were getting stuck in it by the new time.

Patrons were calling me saying, 'here Billa, I can't get me money back.'

I told them truthfully that I knew nothing about the cigarette machine as I was only in charge of the cabaret. Donie O'Brien turned to Pearse Moore and said, 'here kid, you're making more out of that machine than the cabaret.'

When Bishop Murphy died, just after the North Cathedral was blessed and re-opened, my grandson Jonathan rushed home from school all excitement, telling his mother, 'we have no school tomorrow.'

'Why not?' she asked

'Because Shepherd Murphy is dead.'

I was telling this to my good friend, the parish priest of Ballyphehane, an tAthair Ó Mathúna and he told me another story about Bishop Murphy. He was saying his prayers next to the remains of Bishop Murphy in the coffin, when an elderly Cork lady came in to pay her respects. Seeing an tAthair Ó Mathúna she said to him, 'isn't he lovely Father?'

'He is indeed Mam, he's really lovely.'

'Do you know,' says she, 'when you see him there like that 'tis a shame to bury him.'

Fr Mathew, the spiritual director of the well-known Father Mathew Hall, held an annual Pioneer Rally which would always be sold out, God be with the days. The story goes that Fr Mathew had been standing by the box office in complete control of all that was happening when a man approached him – all the worse for the weather. The poor man was so bad he didn't know whether he was at Fr Mathew Hall or the bus office. Fr Mathew took him on straight away, lifting up the cord he had about his waist, saying as only Fr Mathew could, 'get out of my hall, get out of my hall.'

Your man looked up, saw the bearded Capuchin in front of him and said, 'get away ye jinny goat, you're like our Lord beatin' the moneylenders out of the temple.'

God rest Fr Mathew, he did great work for the hall.

I used to call my first car 'my aga-cooker' – an old Anglia. It never left me down, although it use to burn oil by the churn. I always remember there was a hole in the floor in the back of the car and all of the regulars going to the shows, tried to avoid that side. One night coming home from West Cork after a concert, John R. O'Shea was sitting in the front, with Mary Langan and one of the McTaggart Irish dancers sitting in the back. While I was driving I could hear them fighting, arguing and bickering behind. I turned around and said in a very definite way, 'if ye won't shut up, I'll put the two of ye out of the car, and ye can walk home.'

One of the them replied, 'we'd have more comfort any-way.'

Hard to blame them with fumes and water lashing around them, but didn't I get my answer?

West Cork Humour

To say I love West Cork does not mean I have anything whatsoever against East Cork, but if you go to a certain place for forty years or more you feel that place, and see it clearly in your mind's eye. It becomes part of you. I love returning to the Warren in Rosscarbery with my seventeen grandchildren and when I play now with them in the wet, soft sand, and run with them away from the rushing tide, I'm playing with the memories I had of my own children. Grandchildren are a double blessing. You have fun at an age when you should be serious. I can be a boy again, and pretend I'm amusing my grandchildren. I can tell my own daughters I'm giving them a break, to have time with their own mother, but the truth is I'm in my second heaven. My little audience would be so happy and so full of enthusiasm, I would want to give them a round of applause when I would hear the chant cry out, 'Come on Granddad, come on Granddad, let's go across the channel.'

All seventeen of them would have waited and waited for the tide to be out far enough so that we could all hold hands, make a chain, and set off across the wet soft sand, step by step to the Pier Road on the far side. With this great adventure I would get help from my sons Bill and Chris and my sons-in-law John and Paddy and proud leader himself, our dear dog Ben. Ben would race ahead to find the shallow side, trot back and forth and watch them all until the very last child had gone clear of the water. Ben was the best dropped pup this side of Shandon Steeple. He was a cross between a blonde labrador and a red setter, yet he was as black as the ace of spades, but a faithful friend, true and true. When he had to be put down we nearly had a wake.

During the summer months now I watch the weather forecast with a childlike stare, because I know that if the weather is right we will all ring each other. Mary, Judith, Valerie, Carol-Ann and Bill and down west we will drive to our Warren in Rosscarbery, with screaming grandchildren sampling Granny's food, while she lies stretched soaking up the sun. Then we would stoke up a barbecue, with sausages sizzling, children shouting over sandwiches, coke and orange juice. What more could I want! Not to mind Christmas day with these self-igniting candles, stuck in my birthday cake and me huffing and puffing trying to blow them out, and they singing full throttle 'Happy Birthday dear Granddad'. Do you know what – the adrenaline flows as if I was getting a standing ovation in the Opera House.

Back to West Cork and the reasons why I love it so much, apart from the beauty of the mountains, the heather and gorse and the wild open seas. It's the people, and the way they say things – the angle they can put on a sentence – it is a different language entirely to Cork City, different humour altogether.

One year during my holidays, I met Connie Fitz. He hadn't seen me for awhile and I must have put on weight because he took one look at me and said, 'by gor Billa, but you're thickening.'

Connie was very thin and gaunt, always wearing a peaked cap. At the time we had a dog called Major, who was very old and very fat. One morning at the creamery – I used to take my own children on Bill Harte's donkey to the creamery and they loved it – and while Major was wobbling around, one of the locals asked Connie, who had arrived in his donkey and butt, 'Connie, who owns that dog?'

'Have one look at the size of him,' says Connie, ''tis easy to know there's nobody around here owns him anyway.'

Now it is fair to say Connie's only means of transport had been his donkey and butt. A neighbour who died left his donkey to Connie so he felt very well off, being the owner of two donkeys. A local farmer went to buy the second donkey from Connie, but Connie wouldn't budge, for sentimental reasons I suppose. The farmer kept tormenting Connie and said to him, 'in the name of all that's good and holy, what do you want two donkeys for?'

'You'd never know,' says Connie, 'spare parts.'

The farmer gave up after that.

Another night, we were up in Peg Hodnett's bar, at the top of the square. Connie had been at a funeral, and was talking about the woman who had died with Peg.

'How old was she?' asked Connie.

'Ninety-four,' said Peg.

'By gor,' says Connie, 'didn't she reach a great quota.'

Another feature of this loveable character's lifestyle had been the fact that he had no power whatsoever in his house, only an oil-fired primus and an oil-fired lamp. One morning I was at the creamery as usual. It was at the height of the petrol shortage during the time the Arabs had got together to limit the supply of oil and raise the price. There were queues of cars outside every garage in the country. Connie arrived on his donkey and butt, raising aloft his small gallon tin drum, shouting out to Con Hodnett, as he waved his little tin drum in the air, 'how are the Arabs behaving lately?'

Could you refuse him? Connie always had the answer or a statement that won you over and left you smiling. It is a gift they have.

I was in a pub another night at about two o'clock in the morning and the publican was shouting at us to get out. One of the locals turned to me and said, 'what time is it Bill?'

'Five to two,' I replied.

'Five to two,' says he, 'isn't it independent she's getting?'

The West Cork answer leaves you hanging up in the air. It is full of innocent drollness. It is full of fun and playfulness, not in any way offensive. It comes straight out of a warm heart, leaving you with no alternative but to laugh. I found myself being irresistibly drawn towards these people, who are not caught up in status symbols or climbing the social ladder. They are themselves, true and true. Take for example the McDaniels roadshow that used to visit Rosscarbery on an annual basis. They used to put on a different show every night in Hodnett's Hall. One night, when they had finished *Noreen Bawn,* a member of the cast came out on stage to thank the people of Rosscarbery for their support. He invited them to come again the following night because they were putting on a show called *Annie Oakley.*

'In other words,' he said, 'we will bring all you kind people of Rosscarbery away out west.'

A voice rang out from the back of the hall, 'dá flaitheas Dé, but will you bring us back again!'

Now there is honest to God playfulness. Country folk away out west have their own way of saying things. They also have a very unique way of giving directions. Everything is north or south, east or west. Fr Con Cottrell, a Rosminian priest and an old friend, told me he was saying Mass in Ballingeary. He had glasses for reading and he asked the altar boy to put them out on the altar before Mass. Just before going out, Fr Con asked the young lad, 'are my glasses on the altar?'

'They are east of the tabernacle Father,' the young lad replied.

That kind of an answer would put me off my prayers.

As they say, there is no telling what would come out of them next. What do you think of this comment, coming from a man on his death-bed? You may be forgiven for thinking it is something religious, something to do with the spirit, the soul on its final journey, a vision perhaps. You couldn't be further from the truth. Fr John Egan, also a Rosminian priest, went to administer Extreme Unction to a farmer around the Upton area. At the solemn part of the anointing, they heard the snap of a rat trap go off. Despite being on his death-bed, he called up to the kitchen, 'Katie, Katie, we caught the bastard.'

Now in my opinion, under the circumstances, that is a display of pure faith, and absolute confidence in God's mercy.

I became great friends with Fr Con Cottrell, Br Joe O'Brien and many others. We used to take the pantomime to Upton. I had become involved in the Bingo and the Steam Rally on an annual basis, and the Drishane Nuns had joined forces with the Rosminian Fathers, to help the handicapped. But don't think for one moment that all day every day was all very serious with these priests and brothers. They were well able to play a practical joke on each other, like the day Fr Con Cottrell decided to round up about two hundred young fellows and send them to confession. It was the Thursday before the first Friday of the month and had been a beautiful warm summer's evening, Fr Michael Fern was sitting in his confessional box, not doing much business when in the boys started coming, one, two, three. One young fellow was due for his First Holy Communion, and at that time young lads had to have two trial runs before their final confession, making three trips in all into the confession box.

Poor Fr Michael was exhausted from the heat, the confined space, and the grid to the left, the grid to the right. In next came a small young fellow nearly ready for his First Holy Communion, and the whole church heard that innocent voice proclaim, 'Father, this is my last confession.'

Do you know something, I think West Cork humour begins at the Viaduct, just outside Bishopstown, young or old, they have a saying for everything.

Speaking of confessions, I had an experience myself in a confessional box. I related it to a West Cork man during my holidays and going to confession will never be the same again for me. I should have kept my mouth shut. It was just before Christmas a number of years back, my wife, Nell, had some shopping to do and I had to do a radio chat with RTÉ Cork Local Radio about the pantomime that would be starting in the Opera House. I told Nell the best place to meet would be in the Holy Trinity church, and while I had been waiting for her, a clatter of priests came out to hear confessions.

'Now is my chance,' says I to myself, 'to get confession for Christmas.'

I went to the nearest priest, and when I went into the room I found myself face to face with him. I sat down in front of him and I opened my heart and soul as best I could and told him all my sins. When he had given me my penance, there was a slight pause and with a lovely chuckle he says, 'tell me Billa, how's the pantomime going over?'

'We're flying Father,' says I.

'Have a Happy Christmas and I'll be in to see you later.'

It was a lovely experience. I never forgot it. It is one I will always cherish; but when I told all this with genuine sincerity to my friend in West Cork, he kept staring me as I spoke, as if he was hanging on to every word. When I finished, and he says to me, 'did you say you were face to face with this priest?'

'That's right.'

'And was it pitch black?'

'No, no, no.'

'Do you know what Billa, I would rather face a black bull in bad temper, than face a priest like that.'

You can appreciate now every once in awhile when I go into a pitch black confessional box, I see this big black bull in bad temper in my head, and it puts me off my stride for a little while, but I'm very quick to recover. West Cork people have this wonderful visual side to their sayings, and sometimes they themselves don't realise the rich humour in them.

CORNMARKET STREET

I love this old street. I often stroll down it to meet old friends. It once was a channel, imagine that. The carpet and furniture place called 'The Loft', was built in famine times and believe it or not, the famous Don Juan de Aquila once strolled down Portney's Lane, off the Coal Quay. The same Don Juan had been the commander of the Spanish forces during the Battle of Kinsale in 1601. Answer me this – what was he doing down Portney's Lane? No wonder we lost! I suppose he was on the run from the English, and let me tell you, no better place to get protection. However, my purpose strolling down the Coal Quay would have very little to do with the Battle of Kinsale or the Flight of the Earls. It would have a lot to do with just meeting Peggy Twomey at the Bridewell corner, the attractive Murray girls, always in good humour ready for the banter, and Nellie Brady, next door to Annie Punch, who no longer sells behind the little door. And what about Bridgie and Christina, still selling away, hale and hearty to this very day, come rain or shine. They have a stall across the road from the Roundy House Pub on the corner of Castle Street.

Such an atmosphere brings to mind a story of a very posh gentleman, who had been dining at the Oyster Tavern on Christmas Eve. It suddenly dawned on him that he had forgotten to get his Christmas tree. At around three o'clock in the afternoon, he trotted across Patrick Street heading for the Coal Quay. The first two stall-holders were tidying up, completely sold out. One of the women saw that the gentleman was a bit upset.

'Have you a problem sir?' says she.

'Oh,' says he, 'I do have to get a Christmas tree. I simply could not face my good lady when I get home without a Christmas tree. Is there any way you could assist me?'

Her assistant in the stall, wondering what happened, shouted down, 'tell me, what's wrong with him?'

'He's not well,' says she, 'here he is at three o'clock on a Christmas Eve, looking for a Christmas tree.'

'Don't make me laugh,' came the reply. 'Little boy 'tis Easter eggs we're selling now.'

The gentleman could only let his mouth fall open, and make a quick escape.

You'll get your answer down the Coal Quay, that's why I used love covering it long ago, six days a week, when I was with Thompsons. I could hear the heart of Cork beat loud and clear with what they said, and how they said it. All of them are friends of mine to this day, and I would not wish it any other way. No wonder I never had to buy an Easter egg for the children or a Christmas tree at Christmas. That's the type of people you have down there. Hearts of gold, characters all.

One of the many characters was a lady by the name of Annie Punch, who had a shop and a stall right in the centre, where the Paintwell Company is now. Well, I had three little girls at the time, and we were expecting our fourth baby. I told Annie Punch we were expecting again. Naturally, she said, 'I hope Billa, for you and for the Mrs, that this time 'twill be a change, a little boy would be nice.'

When the event happened, it was another little girl. When I told Annie we had another little girl, Carol-Ann, Annie called me aside and said, 'I want you now boy,' says she, 'the next time you go about your bit of business, to put your cap on, and face Shandon.'

She told the truth. I took her advice and had two sons later, Bill and Chris. When I related that story on a *Late Late Show* with Gay Bryne, it came across very well. As I had mentioned Annie and the Coal Quay, I went down a few days later looking for her, only to be met by her daughter, Joannie.

'Joannie,' says I, 'I hope your mother didn't mind me mentioning her on the *Late Late Show* with Gay Byrne.'

'Mind boy,' says she, 'did me mother mind, did she mind? She is so over the moon because of it, and everyone saying it to her, she didn't go in from the front door since.'

Another day while delivering my cakes, I came across a slice of warm humanity I never forgot. I had been delivering to Peggy Twomey and the shop was packed. The conversation was about a young man in the Bridewell across the road who had been detained on a very, very serious charge. The remarks about him were far from nice.

'Jail isn't good enough for him. I'd love to kick him you know where.'

In the middle of all this Peggy Twomey called me aside

and said, 'Billa boy, there's a child over there in the Bride-well, nobody wants him, but he's some mother's child, so go to your van, get me a dozen of Thompsons best, and I'll send them over later.'

That very simple gesture made a deep impression on me. People who do wrong and commit serious crimes are not undeserving of human sympathy They are not beyond the reach of a kind act and they present an opportunity to the rest of us to do just that. Peggy Twomey did it, out of her good nature. She didn't want anybody to know, or did not want any glory or her photograph across the *Examiner*. A woman of substance – I admire that.

I have equal admiration for another lady down in Kyle Street. Big hearts are rare, but when you meet one, your view of life can change forever. A person with soul and spirit can shine out at you, and leave you staring in disbe-lief. For many years Miah Lynch, others and myself, used bring young boys out from St Patrick's Industrial School in Upton to stay with friends of ours, just for Christmas Day.

They used arrive in Cork City in motor-cars, and in a lorry, and they would be collected late that night. It was the one day they looked forward to with excitement and high spirits. You know the kind young boys are, and the lively way they have for showing joy to the rest of us.

A few of them were given out amongst friends in the Coal Quay, and late that Christmas night when Miah went with the lorry to collect the gang, Brother Harry Johnson, one of the Rosminian Brothers, was with him. 'Off you go there, Brother, down Kyle Street with you; you know the woman, she has nine children of her own.'

When he knocked on the door, and asked for the young lad from Upton, the answer was, 'Brother, I know I have a large family, sure one more won't make any difference.'

She wanted to keep the boy from Upton. She would have, and a mother to that boy she would be, as if that boy had been one of her own. These women are truly the unsung heroes of our city. While I have many memories of the Coal Quay, memories full of humour and fast wit, somehow the cakes for Peggy Twomey and the little boy from Upton, who nearly found a home, have a special place in my heart, and do you know why? They have made a difference to me in my life; they have made me think about the things that matter, and that can't be bad.

Rocky Road of Show Business

There is no business like show business. I can accept that, but while it is a happy business, it has its moments too. I suppose you can't please all the people all the time. You win some, you lose some.

I did a show for Showerings, a factory outside Clonmel in County Tipperary. I went on with the wig as Maggie Murphy and died a death for twenty minutes. Half-way through I thought of the old Tipperary saying, 'the hay saved and Cork beat'. The Tipperary crowd are getting their own back I said to myself. Christy Ring had their hearts broken at the time. I imagined I had suddenly become their sacrificial lamb on the altar of entertainment. I did Maggie Murphy in my revved up Cork twang. They must have thought I was from outer space. I had lost it. They were looking up at me blankly. I was ready to shout at them, 'what in God's name brought me down here to Clonmel with this Cork accent?' I couldn't wait to get off. Only for the song at the end of my act, I would have asked God to take me!

I changed, got into my suit, went to the bar and had one pint before heading for the safety of my native county bounds outside Mitchelstown. As I nursed my pint, I was feeling very down and I heard a fellow next to me say to his friend, who didn't recognise me without the wig and make-up, 'wasn't your man from Cork brutal?'

Even the fellow that booked me had been so embarrassed he sent a complete stranger to give me my money in an envelope. I can tell you, I finished my pint fast, put my hand on my money, muttered under my breath 'Up Cork', said goodbye to Sliabh na mBan, Knocknagow, the homes of Tipperary, John Doyle, Jimmy Doyle, every Doyle. When I crossed the county bounds that night, I burst into 'On the Banks of My Own Lovely Lee'. I still remember the relief, I was like an emigrant returning from a foreign country.

However, it must be said fortune favours the brave. On the other side, I remember doing a show for Fitzpatrick Hotels, a golf classic, held by the Fitzpatrick family in the Shannon Shamrock Hotel in Shannon. This time I had been telling a few stories about Cork humour, and as they say in the business, I was having a blinder, thank God. I was playing with the wind. During my jokes there had been plenty of applause, plenty of laughter, which I admit, is a great feeling. But there was one fellow who had been heckling me from the word go. As I was doing so well I decided to ignore him, let him off. But during the course of one of my stories I told the audience I worked for Beamish and Crawford in Cork. Our big mouth, trouble-maker, shouted up from his table, 'and tell us what do they make?'

Instinctively I stopped. I looked down at him. I held his gaze. A hush had come over the audience and I said nice and easy, 'muzzles'.

A burst of laughter, a round of applause and that was the end of him for the rest of the night. Would you believe I got a booking out of it? The same man came up to me later, shook hands and booked me for his company's next annual dinner!

I can tell you, making humour isn't as easy as some people imagine. To stay focused during heckling is one thing, but to not lose your concentration while your heart is heavy is the most difficult of all.

I remember during one *Up Cork* show my eldest daughter, Mary, had problems with her ears. Dr Delap found she had a mastoid in one of them. When she had the operation both Nell and I had a very anxious week. Her hearing was in the balance. The show had to go on. People pay their money to be entertained. I am expected to be funny. Thoughts of Mary being deaf would flash through my mind, as the audience would burst out with laughter.

Pat Murray, our artistic director, used always say, 'let your troubles at the stage door, and collect them on the way out.' It is easier said than done, because one of the secrets of humour is to reach that punch line at the right moment. My mood and the mood of the audience must be in perfect harmony, and then my gut will know when to deliver that punch line. If my heart is troubled it can come between the audience and me, and it can make me experience terrible stress. The fear alone of it happening is enough to cause panic in my head. In any other job you can get detached for a moment to regain your composure, but not on stage while making others laugh. I feed off how the audience and I interact, and I can't laugh when the audience are laughing, even though laughter is very infectious. When laughter is at its loudest, it is then that I must hold my head, pause, and move on; but the thoughts that can jump into the mind at a crucial moment can distract, and have to be dismissed immediately.

For example, one night at the Boys Club in Bantry, I was with the famous Din Joe and his cast of *Take the Floor*. Now Din Joe, whose real name was Denis Fitzgibbon, was a Corkman from the Currow Road, Turners Cross. He was a big man in every way and drew big crowds everywhere he went. Outside the Boys Club the queues were long and deep. At the box office stood a local character, God rest him, Austin Twomey. He was like the town crier as he roared out: 'Come along, come along, and see the great Din Joe. Come along, come along, and see the great Din Joe.'

Din Joe heard this and said, 'like a good boy, come in out of there, do you think I'm a gorilla at a circus?'

Now picture me on stage later, the crowd nicely warmed up, and I heading for the first punch line in my story. This elderly man in the front row, grey hair, uncombed, no false teeth, picking and prodding and scratching himself. What do you think flashed through my mind? Din Joe and the gorilla comment!

I hit my punch line – laughter burst out. Up his hands went in the air, and he stamped his feet on the timber floor. Do you know what? If only I had the branch of a tree in my hand, I would have lobbed it down on him, and said, 'climb that, and go home ye gorilla, you're throwing me off my stride!'

Another night in Clonakilty Industrial Hall, a thought passed through my head at the crucial moment again. I had driven down with another famous Cork man, Joe Lynch, in his Volkswagen. On our way down a young lad passed us out doing a ferocious speed, and he zigzagged all over the road, which frightened the life out of us. When we arrived in Bandon, the mad driver had stopped. Joe rolled down his window and said, 'the way you're driving, there's a slab in the morgue waiting for you.'

When we got to Clonakilty we were a bit early for the show, so we went for a walk around by the Industrial Hall; and what do you think we came across? I couldn't believe my eyes. There was a horse fettered, with a chain tied to his front and his back leg and both his legs were badly cut and bleeding. His head was drooping almost down to the road, and his two sad eyes had pain hopping out at us. What could we do? It did upset us. Straight away, in fairness to Joe, down he went and reported the matter to the guards. A man after my own heart!

Then on went the show, out on stage I walked, doing my act, but as they laughed that night, thoughts of that poor horse kept flashing through my mind. So, it must be said, there are times when I have to do battle with myself on stage, battle quietly and win the war, or else that warm feeling I adore will turn cold and leave me all distressed and disappointed.

Here is another story about the famous Joe Lynch, an incident really, that re-bounded on me. It happened in Bandon and as usual I was looking at Joe on stage, and marvelling at the way he could always get his audience into the palm of his hand, while speaking on any topic.

There was Joe finishing the show with a tremendous rendering of 'Kevin Barry', with Chris Curran on the piano. When he walked off the stage, the crowd was clamouring for more. I walked on stage as MC and said: 'On behalf of the people of Bandon, I want to wish Joe Lynch good luck, good health, and God bless you, Joe.'

Again, this got rapturous applause. Then, when the show was over, I went back to the Munster Arms with Joe. While we were having a drink beside the reception area an elderly gentleman passed through and said, 'Billa, you are one thundering rogue, God bless you is right, 'twouldn't trouble you if Joe Lynch fell and broke his leg.'

Isn't there always someone out there to keep you humble, to keep you from losing the run of yourself.

The rocky road of show business has its moments of uncertainty, moments when it can all backfire, and leave you with egg on your face – like in Rossmore in West Cork when I announced the winner of a talent competition during festival week. It was a singing talent competition to be exact. I sat in the middle of the hall and I knew none of the contestants. I tried to be as objective as I could. I had been invited down by a great friend of mine, the late Councillor John Cal McCarthy, whom I had met many times at functions in West Cork, while he was chairman of Cork County Council.

When the moment came for me to go on stage to announce the winner, up I went, as they say, and I had my hand in my heart. 'The winner is Maura McCarthy, for singing "The Holy City, Jerusalem".'

A big cheer went up in Rossmore Hall, and I noticed many people started laughing, a few of them couldn't be consoled. I wondered what the joke was. I was informed from the side of the stage that the winner was the wife of none other that Councillor John Cal McCarthy, chairman of Cork County Council! When the cheering and clapping and laughter had finally died down, a voice shot up from the back saying, 'cute boy Billa, you'll be back again next year.'

He was dead right! I was back for many years. It turned out to be one of the best accidental backfires that ever happened to me.

Another night, closer to home, Jack Lynch, the real Taoiseach, saved me. You could say in GAA language, he passed the ball to me, as I stood in front of an open goal, and I turned defeat into victory like a flash. God reward him. He never lost his touch. He had been Minister for Industry and Commerce at the time and I had been booked to do a dinner in the Imperial Hotel. Jack presided as minister. I came on to do my spot, and I died a death. I was very annoyed with myself. I kept going over and over in my head – why didn't I warm up more, change the story half way through, sing a song, and do something, when I felt it slipping away from me.

I sat there waiting for the function to be over. I was half

embarrassed, in front of the home crowd, and the man I admired so much, present. The MC that evening had been a lady. She rang a bell and announced from the top table in a posh voice: 'The minister requests that Billa should do "The Hooley in Ballyphehane".'

I could not believe it. I nearly jumped out of my chair. Up I went with such pent-up energy inside me they did not know what hit them. I had a blinder. In fairness to Jack, God rest his soul, he saved the night for me – a gentleman to his fingertips.

Then, would you believe the following night I had a spot at another dinner in the Metropole Hotel; and lo and behold, who was at the dinner again but Jack Lynch.

I was standing at the reception, ready to pass out as he passed in. 'Goodnight, minister,' I said in a state of confusion. There and then the warmth and humour came out of Jack, despite his important position, as he said, 'Billa boy, I hope you'll be all right tonight.'

Jack always had his finger on the pulse of the people. He was too big for no man or woman, and no man or woman was too big for him. Even in small, little things, Jack had that touch. Like the day my own son Bill met Jack outside the old stand down at the old park. He had been autograph-hunting at the time, and the minute Jack Lynch appeared young Bill beside me bolted like a greyhound in the track. To Bill's delight, Jack said as he flicked through the pages, 'seeing where you come from, and your name is O'Connell, I had better write on a blue page for you.'

That was our Jack to the core. Such an ordinary man who did extraordinary things for our nation. How can we thank him? His life was gentle, and the tears that flowed as his funeral moved down through his native city were tears of sorrow, mixed with 'thank you Jack, you were a gentleman, with exquisite manners, the likes of who we will never see again'.

All those who wept at the graveside, many of whom never met him in their lives, came out that day, to stand up and say to the world, *This was a Man.*

I remember another night, down in the Gleneagle in Killarney, when I did a show for the Creamery Association. I died a death the same night, as they say in the theatre world. On my way over the county bounds, down and out in myself, I realised I had another function down in the Gleneagle the following week with the Garda Annual Dinner – a very big night always in Killarney.

When I arrived, the band-leader himself, Michael O'Callaghan, known at Mr Music, says to me, 'Billa, are you on tonight?'

I told him my story and waited for the moment to walk on.

'Right lads, get ready,' I heard Michael O'Callaghan say.

Spot lights and colour lights began to flash in the semi-darkness. I thought it was Danny Kaye was coming on, I got such an introduction. Then 'The Banks' started up, on I walked, told a joke, the band laughed, then it passed on down through the crowd and I had a blinder. Without Michael that night I would have died again. The old dog for the hard road.

Another aspect of this rocky road is the question of mistaken identity. Outside Connie Donovan's pub in Cattle-market Avenue, two women approached my car and said, 'I was in to see ye last night and I thought the show was brilliant.'

The other woman said, 'who's that boy?' to which came the reply, 'don't tell me you don't know him! The whole city knows him, and if you want a good laugh go in to see him in the Opera House.'

I wished both of them well, feeling full of my own importance after all the praise lavished on me, when the woman who 'knew' me shouted after me, 'good luck and God bless you Paddy boy, and keep up the good work.'

Trust Paddy Comerford to get the praise!

As I always say, you'll never get a big head in Cork. Just to prove my point – I remember before I retired from the brewery, I was asked to cover the mid-Cork area for a few days. I called to this pub and started by saying, 'I'm from Beamish and Crawford and my name is O'Connell.'

The publican cut in straight away and said, 'don't tell me at all who you are my lovely decent man, many is the laugh you gave us in the Opera House.'

He then called his wife and said, 'do you know your man?'

The poor woman was highly embarrassed, because she didn't know me from Adam. I was embarrassed standing outside the counter.

'Well anyway,' says he, 'I know you well, you're Cha and Miah.'

I got my order and had a good laugh out in the street. You can't win them all. Show business does have its ups and downs. I know I learned an awful lot about human nature and about myself from being up there on the stage. Fear is the worst, not fear of the audience, but fear that laughter won't come, fear that you are not in the correct form for the occasion. I'm told the worst fear of all is fear of fear itself.

I remember one particular night in the Imperial Hotel, I had been asked by Donal Crosbie, Lord have mercy on him, to do a show.

'Donal,' I said, 'I know the people who will be at that. They are blue in the face from looking and listening to me.'

Donal being the man he was, I couldn't say no. I suggested I bring John R. along. I explained to John R. I had a terrible doubt about the show; and when I had one look at the function room, I knew my fears were well founded. Talk about fear of fear. At the top table sat Brian Sloane, the Lord Mayor. I turned to John R. and said, panic-stricken, 'I haven't a notion of doing this gig.'

John R. looked at me straight between the eyes and said, 'Billa, don't panic, listen to me now. Do me a favour Billa.'

'What do you mean, do you a favour?' says I.

'We'll do this gig, do you hear me. We'll do this gig, because I want to build a little wall. I have fifty concrete blocks outside in John A. Woods, and that crowd out there are going to pay for them. So for old times sake, go out there and see my concrete blocks across their foreheads; do ye hear me now my lovely boy, concrete blocks across their foreheads, out you go, and go for it Billa.'

Out I went, pumped up and primed up like a ballistic missile. They didn't know from Adam what hit them. I gave them joke and story, story and joke, one after the other; and as they laughed I could see concrete everywhere. Making humour through aggression was like a new art form to me. I discovered when you confront your fears, they fade away like the morning dew. In other situations in life, that experience in the Imperial Hotel stood to me ever after. The book of life is a great teacher, and didn't I learn a wonderful lesson that night.

Sporting Moments

In *Cork's Hurling Story* by Tim Horgan, there is a photograph of Cork's first three-in-a-row All Ireland Hurling Champions 1892, 1893, 1894. On that team was my granduncle, my grandfather's brother, Willie John O'Connell. I say that with pride, not the pride that swells the head, but rather the pride that swells the heart; family pride, the very stuff that keeps us going through good times and bad. When we know our family tree in all its roots and branches, we never get blown over in life. An old saying comes to mind 'as the twig is bent so the tree is inclined', that's the kind of pride that appeals to me.

One hundred and seven years separates Willie John's All-Ireland glory days and my latest grandson, who arrived into this world on 28 August 1999. I would want him to know about his great, great, granduncle, and the Lough, the Barrs, and the Bandon Road. It is part of his little soul, about which he knows absolutely nothing as yet, but his day will come, and he will read of Willie John and his love for the 'beautiful game', the Barrs Club and his native Cork.

He will read too, and be startled just like his father was, and his grandfather before him, of how Willie John died from an accidental blow of a hurley on the head, while training for Cork on 27 April 1897. In *The Story of Champions*, written many years ago by an author who called himself Carbery, a very nice tribute was paid to Willie John O'Connell: 'The memory of Willie John is evergreen around the old cathedral, a great striker, lovely ball player, and who also lived for the game; but fate had it, he also died for the game.'

The name O'Connell is still central to the Barrs and the Lough area. My own son Bill played in all grades of hurling and football for the famous Blues. My late brother Denis was involved for many years on the financial side of things, and when he died his son, Declan, got involved in a similar capacity and is involved right up to this day. My father and Uncle Paddy would follow the Blues to the North Pole if they had to, winter or summer, on foot or bicycle, pony and trap, in sickness or in health. My Uncle Charlie, believe it or not, was the first baby to be baptised in the Lough church on 13 April 1890 by none other than Archdeacon Fleming. Charles O'Connell is the first name in the book. Then, lo and behold, one hundred and nineteen years later, who arrives up to the same church but William O'Connell, the youngest Bill O'Connell of them all.

In many ways, the more things change, the more they remain the same. I still love to see the swans coming over the Lough church, and hear the musical whine of their wings; as in they come to land on the choppy waters of a windy day. I love to see the Blue in full flight down 'the Park', with that sliotar hanging in the air, before it drops down to land, just over the bar. I have no doubt Willie John felt all these things too, one hundred years ago. God rest his soul and all the others with him.

Sport and games have always meant a great deal to me. A Cork person winning an All-Ireland hurling medal or any medal anywhere, anytime, lifts my heart towards the stars. I can sense that mood of drama and theatre tingling in my blood. Even in my youth I felt it and to this day I love the atmosphere at all the matches. Chip vans; stalls selling minerals; people shouting selling programmes; others shouting 'wear your colours, hats or colours'; and the Dunne brothers with banjo and violin, making me sing along gently 'The Banks of My Own Lovely Lee'. In truth I feel I belong, and in that sense of belonging I can let go and shout. I can throw caution to the wind. I can abandon common sense. I can look across the stand and see a priest I know well, an accountant, a pub owner; and they all roaring their heads off just like me. And what do you think has happened? Why all the commotion? A young man from Cork has just hit a small sliotar of a ball into the net with a hurley stick. Blood-red hats and scarves and flags and teddy bears are blowing in the breeze. In a blinding flash, more vivid than lightning, we are all equal; and then the following morning down the Mall, behind the counter, or on the pulpit, we once again put on our masks, and return to our restless daily duties. But the banter lives on, and the game is replayed, and the stories retold.

Then, a few years later, when I meet Pa Joe Ahern, a dentist up in McCurtain Street, and when he says to me with great pride, 'I can still see Tim Crowley in Croke Park, going through the Wexford defence, and a forest of hurleys beating off him' – you understand. You believe. That wonderful image 'a forest of hurleys' revives it all again, and you belong once more.

Likewise, when Jim O'Regan was speaking of Peter Doolan's display at right-full back, in that famous All-Ireland victory by Cork in 1966 – 'anyway Billa,' says he, 'he hits a ball as if he hates it.'

Such a comment makes me feel good for hours.

On a slightly lighter note and not losing sight of the Cork wit in all its subtle swiftness, a story is told about Micka Brennan, one of Cork's great sportsmen of the 1940s. I can still see him with the peak cap and the black knicks, out on the playing field with Sars and with Cork.

He had been invited to play for University College Cork in the Fitzgibbon Cup against Queen's University of Belfast. Within ten minutes Micka had blasted three goals into the back of the Queen's net. The fellow marking him came out in awe of him and said, 'my God, what subjects are you studying at UCC?'

Micka simply replied, 'sums.'

'Twas just as fast as Con Roche when interviewed on RTÉ before the Munster Final, many years after Micka Brennan.

'What do you like about Thurles, Con?' the interviewer asked.

'The road home,' he replied.

Another day, the same Con Roche got a similar answer from Dinny Allen. When I was with Beamishs, I was coming out of the Imperial Hotel and there were my two GAA stars chatting away. When Con Roche saw me he said, 'William, any chance of a Carling umbrella boy?'

Dinny Allen replied like lightning, 'don't take any notice of him, he has more umbrellas than Mary Poppins.'

These are but quips might I say, but they have their place in our daily lives, and should not be ignored or cast to one side. They help us to keep our hearts light. Take the fellow selling water down at the old park on a very hot Sunday afternoon. A local wit got a cup with a torneen fish swimming around in it and he complained straight away: 'Here ould stock, there's a torneen floatin' in me cup.'

Your man says, 'what do ye want for a penny, a salmon?'

Now that's a man with character, a man who is alive, a survivor; life's troubles will never put him down.

Another story with the same edge, the same kind of humorous brinkmanship, is told about what I would call a fanatical Barrs supporter, a 'true blue', the one who would die for the cause. He is very involved in under-age, never without a bag of hurleys, a bag of jerseys, and a clatter of youngsters following behind. The same man would only do his drinking in the Barrs bar, 'twould break his heart to leave his money anywhere else.

One night while at a cabaret in the Barrs pavilion, his wife and himself had words. 'Anyway,' says she, 'you think more of the Barrs than you do of me.'

'Woman,' says he, 'I think more of Glen Rovers than I do of you.'

Say no more, move over in the seat. Don't some supporters risk their lives for the cause?

Once while training with the Barrs for a County Championship match, after a session of hurling and running, the lads were having a shower, and the comments were hopping off the four walls of the dressing-room.

Con Roche jumps out of the shower, all talk, and starts drying himself. He sees my son Bill squirting himself with a body spray. Rochie being on the ball as usual says, 'William, give us a lash off that.'

Bill looked into his gear bag, saw a can of insect repellent, which he uses due to his allergy to insects. He throws the can over to Con and says, 'help yourself there boy.'

There was Con in his birthday suit, shaking the can up and down, by which time all the lads had noticed the switch of cans, except Con himself. Then Con started spraying and sprinkling above and below, front and back, under and over, until he was covered in a mist. All the lads just waited and watched, and in a little while the repellent began to bite. Con began to itch and twitch and curse and roar to the very heavens above.

If St Finbarr didn't come down that night to close the club, he never will. The moral of the story is, never spray anything where you can't scratch!

Another Barrs character was Jim Grady, who came to the Barrs from Cloughdubh at an early age, and gave the Barrs great service, as did his two sons, Dessie and Donal.

One day in Austin Stack Park, Tralee, the Barrs were

playing Austin Stacks in the Munster Club Final. I was with a few of the Barrs supporters including Jim Grady. It got a bit hot verbally between the Austin Stack supporters and us. The cracks were flying high and low, when Grady turned and said, 'get away ye miserable whores, ye didn't even light a night-light for Roger Casement when he arrived in Banna Strand.'

That was the end of the cracks for the rest of the match. I never forgot the spontaneity of it. It's the situation that forces the comment out.

Referees too are not without their quips. Mickey Flaherty of Blackrock is a man I know well, and he can be very witty during a game. One day in Ballinlough during a junior hurling match, there was a fellow taking a side-line ball. Before he took the side-line cut he shifted and placed the ball four or five times.

'Come here,' says Mickey, 'are you playing hurling or pitch and putt?'

Jim Forbes, an officer of the County Board, tells another story about Mickey. One day he arrived a bit late to referee a friendly for Carrigdown and as he ran on to the pitch Jim Forbes shouted, 'you're so late, I think I'll have to report you to our county secretary.'

''Twould be more in your line to go over to Martin Coleman, the goalkeeper, and tell him get out of the goal with his half-door of a hurley.'

Long ago in Sullivan's Quay, a well-known Christian Brother, Henry Somers, was very involved with the GAA and did great work promoting the beautiful game of hurling at under-age level. He had a great turn of phrase. I was at a match one day with him and the referee was doing us no favours. Br Somers and myself kept shouting at the referee to give the young fellows a bit of fair play. The referee eventually came over to Br Somers and said, 'Brother, if you'll open your mouth again, I'll have to ask you for your name.'

'And I'd give it to you, if you could spell it,' Br Somers replied.

Do you remember Jim McCole, who came over from Leeds in England to play for Cork Hibs? He came over in a blaze of glory. On his first Sunday, Flower Lodge was packed. They all came out to see their hero from Leeds, and he did not let the Cork public down. He banged in four goals. I can still see the headlines in the *Cork Examiner*, as it was called then – 'Four Goal McCole' and knowing the Cork public, the name stuck.

Unfortunately for McCole, he didn't get four kicks for the rest of the season, and didn't last too long with Hibs.

Some years later I went into Mick Collins pub in Glanmire, and saw a man at the counter having a drink. While I was talking to Mick, the same man went out to the toilet.

'Is that "Four Goal McCole" that played with Cork Hibs?' I asked.

Like lightning Mick replies, 'the very same man, but

'tis an awful pity he didn't spread out those four goals more.'

A very popular competition in recent years is the Cork City Championship. For the outright winners, there is a fabulous set of watches. Some years ago the Glen and Na Piarsaigh met in the City Final, and so we all know this clash had the best of neighbourly rivalry.

A few days after the final, which Na Piarsaigh had won, I made a call to The Fiddlers Green pub opposite the Glen Hall. While waiting for my order, a Glen supporter and a Na Piarsaigh supporter were hard at it about the match. The Na Piarsaigh fellow kept on building up the game, 'what a game', 'marvellous victory', 'fantastic hurling', while the Glen supporter kept playing it down, 'very poor game', 'very bad standard'.

I could feel the undercurrents of rivalry.

'Anyway,' says the Glen fellow, ''twas only the City Championship, we have the County still to come.'

'Maybe so,' said the man from Na Piarsaigh. 'We have the watches above in the club, and the fellows in the Glen, if they want to know the time, sure they can still look at Shandon.'

Out the door I went with my order, saying to myself, 'long may it live, I hope it never dies.'

Do you remember a few years ago, it took three games to decide the National League Title between Cork and Wexford? I'm glad to say I saw all three. As all GAA supporters

St Finn Barr's National Hurling Club, 1894. Players, back row: *Mick Sexton, Jack Bawn Murphy, Billy Walsh, Tom Horgan, 'Billex' Moloney, Arthur Callanan [sec.] , Willie John O'Connell [my granduncle], Dinny Higgins, Morty Downey, Jack Young, 'Cocker' Foley, sie Kelleher;* front row: *Christy Young, Tim O'Keeffe, Donal Murphy, Tim Murphy, Connie Leary, Jim Harrington, 'Luchas' Leary*

My mother, Julia, and father, Bill, on their wedding day

My wife, Nel
when I met h

Seán Ó Sé

John R. Shea – the Singing Firem

Beamish and Crawford

Acting in As Some Tall Cliff *with* [left to right] *May O'Sullivan, Michael McAuliffe and Lorraine Jones*

Myself with Paddy Comerford in Summer Revels

In Summer Revels *with [from left to right] Michael Twomey, Frank Duggan, Paddy Comerford and myself*

At the Lough – celebrating 50 years as the Dame

With Tony Kenny in pan

Me with Babes in the Wood

ecording 'Beautiful City' in Brian O'Reilly's studio. **Left to right:** *Michael O'Connor, myself and Brian*

My beloved grandchildren

Receiving my Honorary MA at University College, Cork. My son Chris was also conferred with a BA on the very same day, 26 July 1996. Left to right: Carol-Ann, Bill, Valerie, Chris me, Nell, Mary and Judith

At the Civic Reception given by Lord Mayor Joe O'Flynn in April 1999: Left to right: Jack Higgins, city manager, my wife, Nell, myself, Lord Mayor Joe O'Flynn and the Lady Mayores Mary O'Flynn

know, going into Thurles from the Holy Cross side, you always have a guard to direct you into a field. He looked into my car and says, 'Billa, I have a space kept here for you.'

'God bless you,' says I, parking outside the main gate, and thanking the guard as I got out of my car.

'You're the right man, in the right place,' says the guard, 'I'm looking for a copy of the video of the All-Cork *Late Late Show*.'

'No trouble,' says I, 'get out your little black book, and I'll tell you where to get it.'

There we were, chatting away, he writing away, and Cork supporters beside us. As they saw me being booked and spoken to, the slagging started, and up came the shouts, 'about time you were caught', 'about time they put you away'. One voice said, 'guard, put him away for twelve months, and it would be an ease to us all in the city.'

They found it hard to understand why the guard and myself were laughing so much. I thought the slagging had stopped, but on my way in, a hawker from Dublin stopped me and said, in a lovely rich Dublin accent, 'here you are sir, three bars of chocolate for a pound, and each of them the size of yourself.'

I went on a strict diet the minute I came home!

I watched an intermediate match one evening in Carrigtwohill. The corner forward for one of the teams was causing fierce hassle, mouthing off to the referee, upsetting his own players as well. Just on the stroke of half-time, he got a nasty gash on his forehead. As the teams came out for the second half, he was very conspicuous with a big white bandage wrapped around his head like a turban. As he ran on to the field, a wit in the crowd shouted, 'Mickie, take that bandage off your head and stick it around your mouth.'

This vicious side to Cork wit is not strictly confined to the GAA. Another sport, bowl-playing, is very unique to Cork and County Armagh. You know the one, that little ball of iron, twenty-eight ounces in weight, flung down the road, with all the muscle in your arm placed behind it, and all the money in your wallet placed upon it.

Raza's brother, Bert Murphy, was out on the Togher Road with the bowlers, and he placed his last few bob on a score of bowls. To win the day, the man Bert backed had to win the last throw by lofting a bad corner. The bowl went into the dyke in front of Bert. In utter disgust, with his last few bob gone down the drain, Bert lifted his eyes to heaven, saying, 'there's a loft. You could keep pigeons in it.'

Two fellows were in a pub having a pint after a score and one remarked, 'I was on my game today, that last shot was like a bullet, it burned up the road, didn't it?'

With nothing coming back from his buddie, 'well,' says he, waiting for an answer, 'did ye think 'twas fast?'

'Fast me arse, I could read the twenty-eight on the bowl.'

I remember a great friend of my own grandfather, Dinny O'Connell, called Dava Noonan. He was a low-sized heavy man, who wore a plain dark navy suit, peak cap, no collar, no tie, but a striped shirt, complete with front stud. He was the man in the Lough parish for cutting dog's tails. The story goes, to do the job properly he often bit them off!

A life-long friend of his was Tommy Doyle who was the opposite of Dava in every way, right down to the high-pitched speaking voice, whereas Dava had a very big gra-velly voice. Tommy got a new pup and Dava was invited down on Sunday morning after Mass to look at the new pup. He was only waiting to be called on to cut the pup's tail, but to Dava's amazement and disappointment, he found that the pup's tail had already been cut.

While Tommy was waiting for the verdict, Dava had been throwing his critical eye over the animal. 'Well Dava,' says Tommy in a high-pitched voice, 'what d'ye think?'

'I see,' says Dava in his gravelly tone, 'you got his tail cut.'

'I did,' says Tommy.

'And tell me,' says Dava, 'what did you do with the bit you cut off?'

'I threw it away.'

'If you did,' says Dava, 'you threw away the best part of him.'

Dava was a Barrs man to his very soul. Glen Rovers had won eight county finals in a row, and I can safely say Dava captured all the doom and gloom you could ever experience in the south side of Cork City.

When eventually the old enemy had been conquered, and the Barrs had won the County Final, Mok's pub at Fair's Cross, that recognised stronghold of the Barrs, was thronged. Fr Cahalane, who was a curate in the Lough, and president of the Barrs Club for many years, decided on that famous victory night, to go for a late night stroll. It was after closing time, and still great singing and banter continued outside Mok's pub. Fr Cahalane, as he was passing said, 'great day for the parish, Dava.'

'It is indeed, Father, a great day for the parish.'

Fr Cahalane studied Dava a bit more, and said, 'Dava, I think you're merry.'

'I am, Father, and I'm very happy, 'cos I was at the altar of God this morning, we won the County Final this afternoon, and I'm going home now, and I hope I dies tonight.'

Speaking of the Barrs, the Glen and the Rockies, and the great rivalry that exists between them – although it seems to have lost its bite in recent years – I recall a story which captures that bite which often had a bitter taste. It was told to me by John Bennett, a well-known Cork tenor, who also won an All-Ireland hurling medal with Cork in 1966. He was a great Blackrock player. The Barrs and the Rockies were playing in the old park, in the County Championship. Before the match a Blackrock player came into the dressing-room, and started to tog off. His first comment as he took off his coat was addressed to everyone in general: 'I had no tea'.

It fell on deaf ears. Next he took off his tie and said the

same, 'I had no tea'.

It fell on deaf ears again and as he took off his shirt, he repeated once more, 'I had no tea'.

The famous Eudie Coughlan, who had been standing by the dressing-room door, with typical wit, says, 'go out and ate the Barrs will you.'

Miah Lynch tells a story about a next-door neighbour of his who lived in Crosses Green, up from the South Gate Bridge, under the shadow of St Finbarr's cathedral. As Miah says, this lady put God first, then her family and a very close third, the Barrs.

Her house was beside Heaslips Mills, which employed many people from the northside of the Lee, mainly Glen Rovers followers. The Barrs and the Glen met in the County Final in 1946, and the week before you had fierce banter and comments flying back and forth. She was strongly advised by the Glen supporters not to waste her money on the bus – the outcome was a foregone conclusion.

But, as the record shows, the Barrs beat the Glen, and there she stood at her door at five to eight on Monday morning, waiting for her Glen supporters going to work. 'Well,' says she, 'what happened ye yesterday?'

One of the lads from the northside says, ''twas easy for ye to win, ye had divine inspiration with ye, ye had two priests playing with ye, Fr Gantley and Fr Hannify.'

But like lightning she replied, 'once we bate the Glen 'twouldn't trouble me if they were two rabbis.'

Isn't it the stuff that has made Cork hurling great, and long may it last, good old fashioned rivalry.

Take my own granddaughter, down in Ballinlough pitch, at a junior hurling match between the Barrs and Mayfield. Mayfield colours are red. Lisa runs up to me, 'Granddad, the Barrs are playing Cork, who will we shout for?'

'Whoever you like sweetheart.'

'We'll shout for the Barrs Granddad.'

When I recall GAA stories, it would be unthinkable not to have Denis Conroy pass through my mind. Chairman of the Cork County Board, a colourful character, Denis was a loveable rogue.

Loyal Cork supporters, and every lover of 'the beautiful game' of hurling, can still recall, I'm quite certain, that amazing goal by John Fenton from a ground shot. It was pure poetry in motion, and was used later on as part of an advertisement for Liver Fluke. He scored that miraculous goal during a Munster Championship clash in the Gaelic Grounds, Limerick, where Cork had beaten Limerick as it happened.

I was chatting to Denis Conroy after the match and was leaning against the bonnet of my car. This fellow comes up to Dinny, and verbally attacks him saying, 'the tickets you gave me were hopeless. I couldn't see a thing. I couldn't even see John Fenton's goal.'

Dinny, with the hat back on his head, replied, 'what are you complaining about, the Limerick goalie was nearer than you. He didn't see it either.'

Years ago I was asked to do *Fear an Tí* at a dinner in the Victoria Hotel in honour of the late Pádraig O'Keeffe. Páirc Uí Caoimh is called after him. The gentle giant himself from Beara, Weeshie Murphy, was Chairman of the County Board. A great night was had by all and I called on Dinny Conroy for a song. What do you think he sang – 'The Boys of the West Cork Brigade'! How many verses do you think it has? Forty! Dinny started his marathon party piece and after about twenty verses, I tried to cut him. I stood up and said, 'a big round of applause for Dinny Conroy.'

And in his gravelly voice he replied, 'sit down like a good boy, I didn't burn the barracks yet.'

Dinny had a way of his own for being nice to you. When he was on RTÉ radio being interviewed by Marian Finucane, about the famous ban, Marian asked, 'what would you say if your son came in and told you he was playing rugby?'

'I'd ask,' says Dinny, 'who his father was.'

Another day a journalist rang him from the *Cork Examiner*. The journalist wanted him to comment about Ireland's achievements in the World Cup.

'I don't know,' says Dinny, ''tis a funny old game ye are following, when you can get into a quarter final without winning a match.'

There's an answer nowadays to that of course – 'and what about the game you are following. You can get into the quarter final after losing a match and win an All-Ireland through the back door!'

Ger Cunningham stood between the posts for Cork, for twenty years. He stopped some bullets and he stopped our hearts too. One day below in Thurles in a National Hurling League game between Cork and Tipperary, as he ran back to the goal for the second half, a fellow says, 'Cunningham, what have ye two hurleys for?'

Ger smiled at him in his usual genial way, and he ran down to his position, but a wit in the crowd shouts out, 'he has one for puckin' um out, and another for lettin' um in.'

Ger heard the comment and enjoyed the humour.

Speaking of soccer. Do you remember Cork Hibs of long ago? I went into a pub in Shandon Street one day. Hibs had been beaten very badly in a cup-tie by Shamrock Rovers in Flower Lodge.

'Did ye go down to the Lodge yesterday to see Hibs?' I said to the fellow beside me.

'I did in my eye,' says he, 'when I was sick they didn't come to see me.'

I had no answer to that. I remember another occasion where a fellow really got 'one up' on me. It was at a Junior B football match. The Barrs were playing Bishopstown in the Sheandún Cup Final. I'm supposed to be a selector for the Barrs, but to tell you the truth, all I do is look after the water. Before the match, in the dressing-room, we were giving our team every encouragement possible. We were trying to fire them up, raise their blood, get them going. 'Go out there lads, and go for it' – that kind of talk.

I was in pantomime and, for a bit of fun, I said, 'now lads, if we win today, there's a ticket for everyone here for a night at the pantomime in the Opera House.'

A whiz-kid in the corner came out like a shot – 'that's grand and if we lose, we will have to go every night.'

I adore going to the matches, to see my favourite people play their hearts out for a victory large or small. The comments from the crowd give me a lift as much as when Cork scores a goal or a point. I remember one Munster final; Charlie McCarthy, known to us all as Charlie Mac, was 'on song' as they say. He was a wizard with the sidestep, and loved by all Cork supporters.

He got married to Pauline Neff on the eve of a Munster Final, played in Thurles. I was at the wedding which was held in Blarney. Timmy Sullivan, a great Barrs supporter, sat in front of me at the final. When the first ball came to Charlie he dashed out, gained possession, did his little sidestep, one, two, flick of the wrist and blazed it over the bar; pure magic. The crowd went wild with excitement.

Timmy Sullivan turned to us and shouted with his hands in the air, 'I wouldn't doubt ye, Charlie boy, that's one for Pauline, one for Pauline.'

The next ball that broke, Charlie doubled on it, and it nearly hit the corner flag.

'Who's that shot for?' I asked Timmy.

Without batting an eyelid, he turned around and said, 'that shot, that's for the mother-in-law.'

'BEAUTIFUL CITY' CASSETTE TAPE

'Beautiful City' and I go back a long time but I never expected I would end up making a tape with 'Beautiful City'
as one of the songs on it. I'm glad to say it made around
£15,000 for the St Vincent de Paul Society. All I did was
record it and the people in St Vincent de Paul promoted it
and the record shops sold it free of profit.

Singing 'Beautiful City' in Brian O'Reilly's studio in Fermoy is one thing, but singing it in Arbutus Lodge, may I
say is quite a different story, at a doctors' conference no less!
'Beautiful City' is a song I know better than my prayers, but
Brian O'Reilly is a perfectionist, and I had to sing 'Beautiful
City' twenty-three times before he was satisfied. I can still
hear his gentle voice saying, 'Oh Billa, just one more time,
with feeling. Imagine Billa,' he added, 'you are in the Opera
House with a thousand people and you're singing from
your heart.'

There was poor old Maurice Healy on the piano, his
fingers tired from playing it one more time, Michael Cremin
on the drums and he up the walls, and the Polyphonics
weary from ooh, ohs and aah aahs, behind me, as my backing group. Imagine listening to 'Beautiful City' twenty-three
times! 'Tis hard enough listening to it once. After about
eighteen attempts, I went into the recording room one more
time and I turned to Michael Cremin, our drummer, who
was really up the walls by now, tearing the hair out of his

head, and I said, 'tell me Mick, what's the name of this song again?'

Naturally, I can't write the reply, but I can write the reply made to me in Arbutus Lodge, and I'm not sure to this day which is the better one. John R. and myself had been booked to do a doctors' conference. The dinner was running late. I imagine the same type of perfectionism had gone on in the Arbutus kitchen, as went on below with Brian O'Reilly in his Fermoy studio. I suppose the wine hadn't been chilled to the correct temperature, the pheasant needed a little more doing, and the soup needed a little touch of thyme. Make no mistake about it, the food in the Arbutus is the finest in the country.

The doctor who hired us came out of the dining-room, apologised and we went to the bar waiting to be called. There was nobody in the bar only ourselves, when along comes my old friend Tom Kavanagh, a main Ford Dealer in Fermoy. He was with his daughter, who was off to America the very next day, and Tom asked me would I sing an Irish song for his daughter. Could I refuse an old friend? Not on your life, but I noticed as I was singing, people from all parts of the hotel started appearing, and they were mostly American visitors. To cap it all John R. gave a blast of the 'Boys of Fair Hill'.

'Make my night,' says Tom Kavanagh, 'make my night Billa, sing "Beautiful City" for my daughter and all her American friends around her.'

I had to move into another gear with all them Yanks

around. The pride of our little Republic here in Cork was at stake. I threw back my head and gave them a lash of 'Beautiful City, Charming and Pretty' and had them in the palm of my hand before I came to 'My Home by the Lee'. They were dumbfounded but delighted, but just as I finished, Declan Ryan, the then owner and proprietor of our famous Arbutus Lodge Hotel, appeared at the door. 'My God,' he said, 'what do I hear? "Beautiful City" being rendered by Billa. The Arbutus Lodge will never be the same again!'

And there was I, sweat running off me, on a high from the Yanks applauding me, defending the pride of my native city. 'Twas nearly worse than the night I opened the *Echo*, and saw my big bald head in front of me, with recording phones over my ears, and the heading read, 'Billa for the charts'.

'Look at your father,' I said to my young lad, Chris, tongue in cheek, 'I'm going for the charts. Number One in the hit parade. Top of the Pops!'

He took one look at my bald head, and quick as a flash replied, 'you'll fly there, because you have a lot in common with Sinead O'Connor.'

Wouldn't that bring you down to earth fast! How would you answer that?

THE DUNNE BROTHERS

I'm the first to admit every city has its street artists, strolling players and live musicians. But of all the live musicians I have ever heard play, to me the Dunne Brothers were amongst the best. One played the banjo, the other played the violin and one of their favourite spots was outside Roches Stores in Patrick Street. They could play anything and play it in perfect harmony. No wonder people used stand for long periods on cold pavements just to listen to them play.

They were humble men, and very talented. One was very tall and the other was very small. The ate their lunch every day in Mooney's Bar in Cook Street. I often met them there, and it was from there that I booked them for the Country Club, when I had been looking for different acts for our cabaret show. I would collect them from their home in Blackpool, drive them to the Country Club, and return to Blackpool with them after the show. They were easy to work with as they had no pretences and never dreamed of fame or fortune. They were proud of their music and the way they could play it. I would introduce them by saying, 'and here we have, direct from Roches Stores, at enormous expense, the Dunne Brothers.'

The people would shout up from the audience, play this, play that, or whatever. People would be shouting out different popular tunes of the day. It got so difficult for them,

I had to go back on stage and appeal to the people to let them play their own choice. When order was restored, quietness came upon the crowd. Mickey stepped forward to the microphone and said slowly, 'Ladies and Gentlemen, we would like to start with "Carolan's Concerto".'

There was a hush, all mutterings stopped. Slowly the sweet sound of the violin released that haunting melody, capturing instantly the hearts and souls of everybody. Then the banjo started in the background. You could hardly hear it at first, then it got louder, then the violin would fade slightly, and so on they went, weaving in and out of that wonderful tune. You could hear a pin drop as they played and when they finished, the applause nearly lifted the roof of the Country Club. We were all put in our box, and rightly so. Why should any one of us have assumed they could only play simple folk music, or worn out traditional ballads? I will treasure that unforgettable hush, that instant silence, created by the sweet sound of 'Carolan's Concerto', as it sailed out across the audience that night. Mickey and Christy had made magic. It was indeed their finest hour, their moment in the sun. They knew it and responded with heart and soul. They were no longer street musicians that night, no longer looking for a spot to play at the County Final down 'the Park' or at a Munster Final in Killarney or Thurles. They were musicians that night, playing classical music, enchanting their audience. I was delighted for them when the crowd nearly lifted the roof.

Having said all that, I must now also admit I did have

another engagement with the Dunne Brothers, and it was as far removed from 'Carolan's Concerto' as you can get. It was in St Finbarr's cemetery. I had read in the *Examiner* where one of the Dunne Brothers had died. I was naturally saddened because I knew them well, and there I was leaning against my car outside the cemetery, thinking about them, thinking about all the money they had raised for the handicapped out at Upton Steam Rally. When they finished playing they would hand over a substantial amount of their takings to Fr Con Cottrell, who out of respect for them, always allowed them play, even though no hawkers or musicians were allowed at the Steam Rally.

Along comes the big black hearse, pulls up outside the cemetery gates, and out of the main car behind it, step my two boyos, Mickey and Christy.

I heard one of them saying to the other, 'Billa is here.'

As I approached them, they said in astonishment, 'what are you doing here?'

'Out burying one of you two samples,' I replied.

They laughed a hearty laugh, and Mickey said, ''tis me cousin is dead, that was a mistake the *Examiner* made.'

I was looking foolishly at them, when Christy turns round and says, 'you won't get rid of us that easy!'

And off they went behind the coffin, leaving me, as they say, with egg on my face. God rest them now. They were part of our city, and that's important to me.

THE OLD OPERA HOUSE FIRE

Up it went like a box of matches – one of the oldest Opera Houses in Europe. The stage, the galleries, the pit, the dressing-rooms, all destroyed, reduced to rubble and ashes. The heat broke the windows in the School of Art nearby. Traffic jams stretched all the way down Lavitts Quay, Merchants Quay and Patrick Street, buses were held up, and the fire brigade lost equipment in their efforts to quench the blaze.

It happened on 12 December 1955. I had been booked to play *Sleeping Beauty* and I was there that night rehearsing with Paddy Coughlan, Josephine Scanlon, Chris Sheehan, Paddy Cotter, Rita Dwane and many others. We could only move out and watch with horror as the flames lit up the Christmas sky that night. The home of music and song burned like a giant bonfire, leaving that very imposing curved entrance looking down on a heap of rubble. It smouldered for days. That smouldering rubble seemed to capture that sense of personal loss many felt during the weeks and months that followed. It was gone; and for me it was gone in more ways than one.

It was a personal loss for me. I was married on 20 September that same year, and like all young married couples at the time we had to start from square one; meaning, we had the bedroom furnished and the kitchen. I was about to make my first appearance in the old Opera House and I was booked to play for six weeks. My young and charming wife had put her eye on a nice suite of sitting-room furniture in Roches Stores. The money from *Sleeping Beauty* would pay for the furniture. Everything in the garden was rosy.

I arrived home late on that fateful night and Nell had been wondering why I was so late. I brought her to the window. The sky had a deep red glow, reaching away up towards the stars. I said nothing and my wife, being the romantic that she is, gazed in awe at what she saw; then burst out with this wonderful observation, that has gone done in family history, 'Oh Bill,' she said, 'isn't that beautiful? Isn't that the loveliest Rooley-Booley-Alice in all the world?'

'Rooley-Booley-Alice my arse,' says I, 'that's our sitting-room going up in smoke.'

STRANGE LINES

You can learn your lines, repeat them to yourself as you walk down the street. You know you know the script in all its detail, and yet there comes a moment when impulse makes you say something you never intended, and it's the loudest laugh of the night. The audience never sleep, they are with you in every word you say.

There was a scene in *Jack and the Beanstalk* where the bad Baron and his two henchmen come into the Dame's kitchen to plant a bomb. I then used to come in and catch them in the act, but their excuse would be that they were only helping to bake a cake, and the cake was in the oven. At every performance there would be a huge cloud of smoke, followed by an unmerciful loud bang. I would chase the Baron and his two henchmen around the stage with my brush, and clear them out the kitchen door. My son, Jack, and his girlfriend, Jill, would rush on to the stage and they would be all excitement. Jack would say, 'are you all right Mother, I heard a loud bang.'

One night there was plenty of smoke but no bang. Jack ran on, holding Jill's hand, still excited and concerned and said, 'are you all right Mother, I heard a loud bang.'

Spontaneously I replied, throwing a glance at the audience, 'may God bless you, boy, but you have marvellous hearing.' It was off the cuff. It got the loudest laugh of the night. I couldn't resist.

Another night in a different pantomime, Paddy Comerford played the part of a cat, and naturally if you play the part of a cat, there are no lines to be spoken. I missed an entry on stage. I left poor Paddy as the cat on stage all on his own. He couldn't speak. All he could do was prance to the wings and say under his breath in panic, 'meow Billa, meow Billa'.

Straight away, through the intercom backstage, came the stage manager's voice, 'Billa on stage immediately, Billa on stage immediately.'

I rushed out of my dressing-room, took the stairs four at a time, rushed on stage. Instead of starting up my dialogue with the cat, all I said, with my hand on my heart, was 'sorry Paddy.' The audience burst into laughter, and it took a good few minutes before we all settled down again.

But do you know what, I have no pity for that fellow Comerford, prancing about on his own. The things that man has said to me on stage, lines no audience has ever heard, are enough to lock him up for life. Imagine the scene, *Summer Revels* in the Opera House. One particular sketch was called 'The Fords Box'. I played Madgie Murphy and my husband was none other than Paddy Comerford. As the scene opened, fifteen children strolled out of the Fords Box, where we were living. Then Paddy, the father of the fifteen children, struggled out after me in a very exaggerated, exhausted condition. Visually, it was a very strong sketch, and the audience would go into uproar every night. During the laughter, when no lines could be heard, I'd get an earful from Paddy – 'Madgie, put your hand down, and close me flap.'

Another night during the same sketch I got, 'Madgie, call the plumber, the boga is blocked.'

Another night, 'Madgie, any chance of a half-hour with you?'

How did I work with him!

But there is another side to Paddy too, a soft side, a warm human side. In a story he tells about his mother, you'll see what I mean. She always loved watching her boy Paddy on stage in the Opera House. She used go to *Summer Revels* and pantomime nine or ten times, and thought Paddy never knew she was there so often. Paddy always knew the nights she would be there as she would leave her coat lying out on the bed, and she would keep on reminding him, 'Pad, you'd want to be going, or you'll be late.'

Then, when her official night came to go, she would tell him, and would put a sting in the tail by saying, 'anyway, I'm only going in to hear Billa singing.'

The years passed by, all too quickly, and when she was in her middle eighties she had to go to hospital. Paddy was loyal and true to the end. He visited her regularly and would say to her, 'how are you Mother?'

'How do you expect me to be,' she would reply, 'when they put me in here with a pile of old people?'

Couldn't you see the twinkle in his eye and he telling you that one!

But wait until I tell you what he used to do to my son

Chris. Have no doubt Paddy Comerford is a master mischief-maker. During that time the famous Billy Boyle came over to Cork from the West End of London. 'I can sing, I can dance, I'm Billy Boyle' was his catch-phrase and it was the slogan over his photographs, which were plastered all over Cork, promoting the pantomime *Cinderella*. During the pantomime, he would bring young children up from the audience to have a chat with them. My own son Chris, who was around four years of age at the time, practically grew up backstage with all the Opera House staff. He was very obvious, with a big head of curly hair, and Paddy used to slip him in stage left, to join the children from the audience.

Chris would always be first to be interviewed by Billy. He would ask Chris his name. As proud as punch he'd reply, 'Chris'. Then Billy Boyle, knowing who he had, would say, 'what's my name, Chris?'

Naturally Chris would say out loud and clear, 'Billy Boyle.'

The audience were always impressed that a boy so young would know the famous Billy Boyle all the way from London. Billy then would tap Chris on the head, and move on to the next boy, leaving Chris on his own standing stage left.

At that precise moment then, our thundering rogue Paddy Comerford himself, would give a muffled shout from the side, 'go on Chris, do your dance, do your dance.' Chris would proceed to do a bit of a shuffle, upstaging the famous Billy Boyle, delighting the audience. Needless to mention,

Paddy would have got lost backstage somewhere, in convulsions with laughter, leaving me to explain it all away as innocent. But at the same time I'd defend my young fellow too. You can't let down your own, West End of London, Carnegie Hall, or Albert Hall, or any hall!

Paddy Comerford is some character to work with.

Theatrical Friends

I can say one thing about my friends in the theatre and, as they say, I can say it without fear of contradiction. Each one of them is a bigger ball-hopper than the other. Two such characters were Paddy Cotter and Donie Scannell. To us, Donie was the blind boy. He was an accordionist who did many a show with me. He was always treated as one of the boys, and wanted it that way.

One night we did a concert in the convent in Crosshaven for a nun's jubilee. Having brought Donie to the toilet we had to walk back a long corridor. I saw Paddy Cotter coming against us and I whispered to Donie, 'watch it now, there's a priest coming.' Then I said, 'goodnight Father', out loud.

'Goodnight, Father,' Donie added.

Paddy stopped, put his hand on Donie's shoulder and said, 'goodnight my child, and may God restore your eyesight, and if he does you are out of show business.'

Donie recognised who he had, and such was our friendship no offence was taken.

He was always billed as the 'Blind Boy' even though he was nearer to thirty-years of age. He would know where he was going by the slightest touch. You would ask at times, was he blind at all? Like the night in Rosscarbery, we were backstage and a lot of Rosscarbery people were watching Donie walking around in a normal fashion. Bob Carlisle, who spoke with a rather posh pound-notish accent, turned to Donie and said, 'Donal, they are all watching you, like a good man would you walk into a door and prove your point.'

He never took offence. He could return the remark and would surprise you, as he did from the back seat of Donal Kenneally's old Volkswagen when Donal crashed into a bridge near Dungourney. The blind boy got the fright of his life and shouted, 'Oh Goddie, oh Goddie, what's happened?'

Kenneally says, very annoyed, 'I'm after running into a bridge,' and the blind boy's reply was, 'I can see that me-self.'

There was one thing the 'blind boy' hated with all his soul and that was being fed by anybody, especially a nun. Not that he had anything against nuns; it was just that they were so caring and so fussy, and so concerned about him, he used to get all nervous and fretful. He was in such a condition one night and I decided to play a practical joke on him. May God forgive me, I'll never get to Heaven.

We used to bring our pantomime to the South Presentation convent every year, and naturally we'd get a lovely supper afterwards. The nuns would be falling over Donie, telling him what a great boy he was. When it was time to go home the reverend mother went to put on his overcoat, only to find 'twas full of the best silver spoons, silver knives and forks.

'Sister, don't blame me at all, blame Billa, he never leaves me alone,' says Donie in a panic.

I hope he has forgiven me! Often I'd cut his grub for him, gave him the fork, and away he'd go.

His father owned a pub at the top of Shandon Street called Our House. Anytime I go up that street, I can still see him in my mind's eye; the blind boy there in the middle of Shandon Street, at three in the morning, himself and his accordion. That's where I used to drop him off after the shows. One night we were returning from a concert in Bantry and Paddy Cotter was with me. Even though Paddy was a pioneer, he kept annoying Donie all night long during the journey home saying, 'bring us into Our House for a drink, Donie.'

'Cotter, I can't, boy; 'tis too late; 'tis far too late.'

When we got outside Our House, Paddy said for a prank, 'Billa, stop the car, let him find his own way home.'

I cut off the engine, we put his accordion out at the top of Shandon Street, and freewheeled the car a few yards away down the hill, at three in the morning. We stopped the car and looked back, only to see Donie with his certain touch, collect his accordion, go straight to his front door and open it. He turned and waved, and we waved back.

'Blind me arse,' shouted Paddy, and we could see him laugh.

God rest them both, I have lovely memories of them.

John R. O'Shea is one of my closest friends in show business. I have travelled many miles with this man. He was known as the singing fireman, John R. As a true Corkonian, his pedigree is beyond question. No Corkman is more entitled to sing 'The Boys of Fair Hill' than John R. Why might you ask? Well there is a line in the song that says 'when you hear the Shea boy say, Timmy Delaney won the day, here's up them all said the boys of Fair Hill' – the Shea boy was John R.'s uncle, and Timmy Delaney his uncle on his mother's side. Surely there's no one more entitled to sing it than him!

If ever you could say 'he has no enemies' you would be speaking about John R. He always drinks in quarts and always says when he lifts a pint, 'that the Lord may leave us the mind we have for it.'

You couldn't fall out with a man of his nature.

The pair of us got a false offer one night after a show in the old Savoy in Limerick. A stranger approached us who claimed he was an agent in show business in Boston. He had a big belly and a gold tooth, and spoke with a rich American accent, one you could cut with a hack-saw. He put a business card into John R.'s top pocket saying, 'I'm so-and-so in Boston, if you are ever over, I would be only too delighted to pick you up.'

We were used to these false offers. John R. replied, 'I'm driving an ambulance in Cork, and if ever you come up around our way, be careful I won't pick you up.'

He went away with his belly between his legs. John R., like Timmy Delaney, had won the day.

We were returning from a show in Liverpool, and we had to travel through the night to get to the boat, and sail for Dún Laoghaire. We had with us a magnificent hamper, given by our good friends in the Irish Centre in Liverpool. Sandwiches, sausage rolls, fruit and sultana cakes, all of which would break the hunger on our journey home across the Irish Sea. As we walked up the gangplank into the ship, we noticed a woman with five very young children, only to be told that her husband had been killed tragically in Birmingham on a building site. We all gave her a hand with the children's buggies, etc.

After a few hours sailing, we felt the pang of hunger. I asked John R., who had the job of minding the hamper, to get it out, open it up, and we would have a nice cup of tea with the food. John R. turned to me and said, 'Willie, I gave it away to that woman.'

He soared in my estimation. No wonder he has no enemies.

Another time when we were touring we arrived at the Liverpool Irish Centre next door to the famous Liverpool cathedral. Seán Ó Sé who had been doing all the driving said to me, 'Willie hop out there. Hold on to that space outside the centre.'

As I stood there guarding the space, a little Chinese man, driving a Merc, got ready to back into the space. Under pressure, I approached his window, and said in my best English accent, 'I'm from British Gas, and we're going digging here.'

He gave me a big smile and drove away very contented.

In due course Seán Ó Sé arrived with the car and parked it. We started unpacking all our gear for the concert and who arrived in the middle of it all, walking down the street, but my little Chinaman. Now I'm not too tall myself, but he was only up to my navel. He gave out stink in broken English: 'I thought you tell me dis space for British Gas Company!'

Now John R., with his very big frame, was always very protective towards me, and he looked in amazement at his good friend Willie, being roared at by a little Chinese man. Over he stepped saying, 'get away before I give you such a who began it, and you'll land in any space you like in Peking then.'

I thanked John R. sincerely, as I often had done before and the answer was always the same, 'Willie boy, I'd give ye me right hand.' A loyal friend true and true, you could not ruffle him.

I remember one night a fellow had some argument with him and threatened he'd sue him for four figures.

'My lovely,' says John R., 'you can't get a pants from a bare arse.'

Case dismissed so to speak. The singing fireman had won again.

This habit he had of drinking this 'quart' used nearly bring sweat out through my eyes; the times he would decide to have it, just before the show or at the interval maybe! Can you imagine being down in South Tipperary doing a show at the end of a seminar for Alcoholics Anonymous?

Can you appreciate being told by the nun in charge that there were to be no stories or songs about drink? I reassured her, and warned the lads about the nun's request to which they replied, 'no problem'.

The seminar was running a bit late. We had arrived much too early so the singing fireman decided he would go out and have his 'quart'. He came back two hours later saying, 'Willie, I had two handsome quarts.'

'You timed it right, John; we are ready to go on,' I said.

Out I went to a front row of clergy, including the Archbishop of Cashel, Dr Dermot Clifford, a row of nuns and all the people of the seminar. I said my few words and then I said, 'to open the show here's the man himself from Fair Hill, John R. O'Shea.'

What was his first song – 'Little old wine drinker me'! I shall leave it to you to think about me facing the nuns after the show.

John R. had an unusual affect on me. His coolness in a crisis never ceased to amaze me. I nearly got killed coming home from West Cork after a show one night. The man who drove us down was very drunk when we started to come home. I pleaded and pleaded with him to let me drive, all to no avail. We weren't long on the road when he lost control, went over a ditch, landed inside in a bog on the roof of the car – upside down. John R. was in the back of the car with another man. I was there stunned. It was like as if time stood still, and everything was in slow motion. I heard John R. saying, 'Willie, cool head now boy.'

I couldn't answer.

'Open your window.'

I obeyed, like someone in a trance, under hypnosis.

'Crawl out of here,' he said, which I did.

The minute we got out, he examined me from head to toe. The professional fireman had come out in him. I thanked God he had been with us, and that nobody was killed, despite the fact the driver had lost a lot of blood.

Another night we were first to come on an accident at Farran, past Mother Kellys. He walked over, forced open the car door and there was a dead man in the car. John took out the body just as the fire brigade arrived; sat into my car and off we drove to Kealkil to a show, as if it was all in a day's work. What a man!

I admire Michael Twomey, this tall, elegant man of Cha and Miah fame, both as a scriptwriter and producer. He understands comedy as regards timing or changing a word to get the full value. He is a perfectionist as I found out. One Sunday afternoon we were having a dress-rehearsal for *Summer Revels*. I had a magnificent entry as Mary Poppins, coming down from the flies, which is forty feet above the stage. It meant that every night I was strapped with a harness, and hoisted up forty feet, as the Montforts went through their opening number.

Michael made sure they did it again and again and again. There I was dangling like a yo-yo forty feet above the stage, when Tommy Burke, the stage manager, stormed down to Michael and said in a stern voice, 'do you realise there's a man hanging up there for the last half-hour, strapped to a harness?'

'My God,' says Michael, 'bring Billa down.'

I was blue in the face when I landed, speechless from pressure. I should have got danger money, hanging forty feet up as Mary Poppins!

Another night the zip on my skirt broke. Thank God I caught it with the heel of my shoe as it began to fall down onto the stage below me. When I arrived down I was holding up my skirt with my left hand as I did my opening piece. The audience nearly had me as the full monty, but I would have had the last laugh. I always wore bathing togs for safety. You never know do you, you never know!

I was put in my box as they say, and no better boy than Joe Mac to do it – Oliver Reed is still looking at us! Oliver died on 2 May 1999. He fell ill in a pub in Malta and died – I suppose, as he would have wished.

I had been invited down to the Hibernian Hotel in Mallow by County Sound Radio. It was a morning breakfast, £10 a head, to begin a National Campaign for little Joanne O'Riordan. The dining-room was full of people and Robert Walsh of County Sound was interviewing me and the famous Oliver Reed was with me, right there in the dining-room. During the commercials, and waiting to go out live, I was chatting away to Oliver Reed, on a high talking to such a famous character. In the middle of our conversation, who arrived into the room but the bold Joe Mac and I said to Joe, 'what are you doing in Mallow?'

Like lightning, he looked up and said, 'I'm down booking you into Nazareth Home.'

The dining-room cheered him to his seat and I clapped the loudest myself. Pure Cork wit.

Paddy Comerford and I shared a dressing-room with James N. for six weeks. No matter how many times Paddy and I tried to better James N. with stories, he always topped both of us.

He was a real cat lover and always kept around ten cats in his house. One night, during the panto, he came in to get dressed and I noticed his lip was bleeding so I asked what happened. He told me he was cleaning his teeth with some peppermint toothpaste when Swannie, the cat, who liked the taste of peppermint, went for his upper lip, and caused it to bleed. We were shocked and thought 'what a strange cat?'

The last week of the show James N. invited myself, Paddy Comerford and Billy Boyle of West End fame for dinner. He had prepared a beautiful meal and we had wine in silver goblets. Then Paddy Comerford started letting on he was the Bishop of Cork, pointing at the silver goblets, as we were drinking out of them, saying to me, 'you're getting the parish of Ballinhassig, Billy Boyle, you're getting the parish of Douglas, James N. you're for the cathedral.'

When the meal was finished, without batting an eyelid,

Paddy asked James N. had he any peppermints.

'I have to be sure,' says James N, producing a jar.

As I was opening the peppermint, Paddy saw Swannie, the cat, dangling off my left shoulder. He looked at me and said, 'whatever you do Billa, don't let that peppermint fall on to your flap.'

Nobody ever got the better of James N., especially when it came to point-scoring and one-upmanship. In one of his visits to the well-to-do gentlemen's clubs of London, the story is told that James N. was having a drink in a relaxed atmosphere. The topic of conversation was about Lord Snowdon and Princess Margaret, whose marriage was having problems at the time. Several of the gentlemen had voiced their opinion of the marriage break-up, when one of them turned to James N. and said, 'well Jim, what's your opinion of the whole affair?'

'Well, I wouldn't like to comment, or give an opinion, because I've only his side of it,' he said.

As a Corkman would say, beat that in two throws.

When I was young and a regular at the Opera House one of my heroes was Chris Sheehan. I can still see him playing the Red Shadow in *The Desert Song*. Years and years later some company put it on in the Opera House, and when I was in the bar at the interval an elderly gentleman came up to me and said, 'well Billa, there was only one Red Shadow.'

Glad I am to say I worked with him in shows and pantomimes for many years. He was a tremendous loveable character and many was the laugh we had backstage with Chris.

When I worked in Thompsons, Chris worked in the Queen's Old Castle, and every morning as I delivered my cakes to Miss Cahill's shop, later known as Theo's Jewellery Shop, Chris used come out for a chat and a few cakes. One morning while chatting away, I could see behind Chris' shoulder the famous Andy Gaw coming up to us. I whispered to Chris, 'don't say a word, Andy Gaw is coming up right behind you.'

Chris' timing was always spot on. Just as Andy got to his elbow, Chris turned to him and said, 'Andy, you're the right man in the right place, have you a loan of a tanner?'

It was the first time Andy was ever tapped and caught in his life! But I would just like to have it recorded – Andy Gaw gave every tanner and shilling he ever had away to children in Cork City. I suppose to the tourist, Andy was probably seen as a homeless vagrant, but to us Corkonians, he was an innocent, loveable man, who roamed the streets winter and summer, never doing harm to anyone. He was simply looked after by his own, and there's something nice about that.

Bill Mahony was a great character, a great actor, one of the best stage drunks I ever saw. He was also the producer of the famous *Swan* shows. He worked in the Cork Pawn Shop at the bottom of Patrick's Hill and I used often call there, when I was in Thompsons, to have a chat. As we all know there are three balls outside every pawn shop, but for some strange reason there was only one ball outside the Cork Pawn Shop. Bill was helped by another man and one day an American visitor looked up at the one ball and said to a lady coming out of the pawnshop, in his American accent, 'it this a hock shop?'

'I beg your pardon sir?' says she.

'Is this a hock shop?' he repeated.

'Oh, 'tis sir, 'tis the Cork Pawnshop.'

'There's only one ball.'

'I know that sir,' says she, 'the other two are inside.'

I had the pleasure of acting in a great Cork play, *As Some Tall Cliff*, by John Power and produced by James Stack. It was a powerful drama about Cork dockers and hurling. Bill Mahony played the lead as an ex All-Ireland hurler and docker. During the dress-rehearsal James Stack had 'Tough Barry', the Cork hurling trainer, present to keep a watchful eye on the hurling side of things.

When the rehearsal was over Jim Stack called from the back of Fr Mathew Hall, saying in his fine theatrical accent, 'Bill, Jim Barry says you're holding the hurley incorrectly, which was right below left.'

Bill Mahony, being very annoyed, turned to the cast, and in a stage whisper said, 'isn't it terrible to listen to that, after all my hurling years with St Anns.'

I played the part of the son in *As Some Tall Cliff*. It was my first straight part and during the show I had an argument with 'my mother' (Lorraine Jones) on stage. I used have to say, 'for the love of God, mother, leave me alone'.

Fr Mathew himself called me to task. 'Do you realise Billa, you're using God's name in vain in that line.' He advised me to say, 'for goodness sake, mother, leave me alone'.

Weren't times different then? The following night I put in 'for goodness sake' and I was reprimanded by James Stack who said, 'Billa, stick to the script, remember who is paying you.'

I did as James Stack had told me and a few nights later I met Fr Mathew on my way in. 'Billa,' he said, 'when the show is over, I'll either buy you a present or a catechism.'

Bill Mahony loved the theatre, and all the fun that went with it. He loved doing sketches, and the sketch with a slight risk in it had its own attractions for him – the one that might go wrong, or the one that might take on a life of its own, if you know what I mean, like the 'Ball of Fire'. The 'Ball of Fire' was a dog, and in every hall in every town Bill Mahony had to borrow a dog, and walk on stage with the dog on a lead. In West Cork he got a loan of a mangy-looking dog, walked on stage and proceeded to sell the dog all through the sketch – that was the story line. This night he was actually selling the dog as usual and the lines ran, 'I tell you Sir, he's a ball of fire, I tell ye, a ball of fire'. There and then the dog lifted his leg and proceeded to perform on stage. A voice shot up from the back of the hall, 'that will out your ball of fire for ye.'

West Cork wit at its best! He enjoyed it as if it had been

part of the original script. Spontaneous comments he would argue had a power all their own. Not that he was without them himself might I add, and equally unscripted might I say, like the comment he threw at a well-known Cork soprano backstage one night in a Muintir na Tíre Hall in West Cork. There we were, getting ready for a concert, and she was going through her songs and her music sheets. She wasn't sure what to sing or what would be appropriate for her audience. She called to Bill Mahony for his advice, saying, 'Bill, "If I Were a Blackbird"?'

'If you were,' says Bill, 'you'd have feathers in your arse.'

'Tis hard to come back from that, five minutes before curtain.

There's another story told about Bill Mahony that capture what we will call the core of the artistic temperament. He was doing a play in the Fr Mathew Hall. The first few nights he wasn't sure of his lines, so it was arranged to have a prompter with the script to help him. As there was a fireplace on the set it was arranged beforehand that Bill would poke the fire anytime he was caught for a line.

Unknown to Bill the backstage prompter was called away and he gave the script to a priest who was standing nearby. God bless the holy man, he hadn't a clue about theatre, scripts or prompting. So when Bill eventually poked the fire, looking for a prompt, the priest didn't know what page, scene or act he had in the play. There was poor Bill Mahony outside, as we say in the theatre, 'dying a death'. He was poking and poking, and nothing coming back. Out of pure frustration, and not realising 'twas a priest was the prompter, he spoke in divers tongues into the fireplace saying, 'you blind whore, you couldn't read the *Echo,* you won't be there tomorrow night.'

The priest claimed after he heard Bill's magnificent flow ''twas like the Litany of the Saints.'

Tony Hegarty is a great Cork character, great company and larger than life. During a pantomime in the Palace, he played the part of the Baron, Paddy Comerford and I played the ugly sisters and Elaine Carlisle was playing in the orchestra pit. Now remember Tony had produced a show for the Inniscarra group in their local hall weeks before our Christmas pantomime. During our run they paid us a visit in the Palace and Tony asked me to welcome the Inniscarra group on the night, which I did.

The following night about half-an-hour before curtain, Mrs Carlisle, Elaine's mother, brought a bouquet of flowers, and asked me to present the bouquet to Elaine as it was her birthday. Tony came in about ten to eight to get ready for his part. When I saw him, as a ball-hop I said, 'you're a very silly man, leaving so early as you did last night, because the Inniscarra group came back looking for you, but seeing you weren't here, they left you this bouquet of flowers.' I handed him Elaine Carlisle's bouquet of flowers.

Tony took the flowers, looked at them up and down, saying, 'is that what they brought me, flowers, blooming flowers?' and with that he hopped the bouquet of flowers off the wall. When I saw the roses and the dahlias banging off the wall, I nearly died. We spent the rest of the night re-arranging Elaine's bouquet of flowers. By the time we were ready to present them, they were like a bouquet of nettles. Do you realise how close to heart failure you put me, Tony Hegarty?

Happy days in the Palace!

One night Seán Ó Sé and myself travelled up to Longford, to do a cabaret for the Vintner's Association. We were told we would have a room to change in, space at the top table, and we were to go on after the last speech. Alas, when we arrived we had no room to change, no space at the top table; the place was packed four or five deep at the bar. We were playing against the wind. Albert Reynolds was Taoiseach at the time, and was guest of honour at the dinner. I was a rep with Beamishs so I had to keep my powder dry, but we were very annoyed.

Seán Ó Sé called one of the organisers and said, 'I hope if you ever come to Cork you won't be treated like us here tonight.'

He defended himself at once by saying, 'you must re-member we have the Taoiseach here tonight.'

'Well,' said Seán, 'that would never happen to us at home, because we're used to Taoiseachs in Cork.'

'Tis no harm to beat these fellows back into their boxes when they get cocky with the wrong people.

Seán tells a good story about the time he was invited to

a cathedral in Germany. It was a centenary celebration and there was a choir backing him, an organist and a conductor. During rehearsals Seán noticed a couple walking up the centre aisle, and he could see the Roches Stores plastic bag. These are from Cork he says to himself and when he stopped singing he heard the woman saying, 'I'm sure that's the Puckar.'

'Not at all, it couldn't be the Puckar,' replied the man.

Coming back down the aisle, the woman looked up again and said, 'I told you, 'twas the Puckar'.

The conductor of the choir turned to Seán and said, 'I think they do not like your music.'

I owe a lot to Danny Hobbs and I admired him greatly. I did many a show with him as a teenager, and his influence on me, from a theatrical point of view, was profound. I was always very proud and honoured when I was asked to do a show with Dan Hobbs. On reflection, I suppose I would have to admit to a certain amount of hero worship, and as a young lad I equally admit to being in awe of names like Chris Sheehan, Bill Rice, Dick Donegan and Eileen Curran.

Dan Hobbs was a neighbour of mine, and when he was too old for travelling around, he recommended me to many a GAA club in the county. I know Dan Hobbs will be remembered by many of another generation, for the clothes shop in Patrick's Street, where you could go up the timber stairs with your father, to buy your hurley and sliotar, and dream of glory days to come. My memories, however, are rich in sentiment, and steeped in pride, all because of his favourite song, 'The Little Shirt my Mother made for Me'. When Danny would finish 'The Little Shirt' on stage he would always produce and show a genuine shirt about the size of a handkerchief. It had always been a part of his act, and always met with great applause. Two days before he died Dan sent that shirt down to me and I still have it. It is one of my proudest possessions.

The nuns in the Bon Secour Home were very good to him during his final days. They called to see him every day at home, until he died, and went to endless trouble to care for him. One day when the nuns had gone, Danny called his wife and said, in his own inimitable humorous way, 'like a good woman, keep the nuns away from me, they are powdering me from my head to my tail, and St Peter won't recognise me.'

What a terrific comment from a marvellous man, before he met his maker. It was typical of him, and typical as well may I say, were his theatrical antics on and off the stage – like the opening night in the Marian Hall, Ballinhassig, when he was in his prime, and I a nervous young fellow, not long on the road, and full of my own importance. There I was in my black tie and dress suit, doing very well as MC. I was doing so well I looked down towards Danny Hobbs for the thumbs up sign. I was like a schoolboy looking for approval, but all he did was point to his trousers' fly and my fly, telling me in sign language that my fly was wide open.

There I was in front of a whole load of clergy and nuns,

including the Reverend Archdeacon Duggan himself, but I was so embarrassed I was afraid to check. When eventually I came off in a bog of sweat, to find nothing at all wrong with my fly, I saw Danny Hobbs coming towards me at the interval with a smile on his face.

'Dan,' says I, 'you really threw me there.'

''Ere boy, 'tis an old trick of the trade, 'twas done to myself years ago.'

He was a mortal rogue to his very fingertips, and I liked him for it.

Dan was always very topical with his material and when Bishop Danny Coughlan was ready to retire Bishop 'Connie' Lucey was standing in the wings as coadjutor bishop ready to take over. In typical Hobbs fashion, he had stories of the two bishops. Bishop Lucey used to visit Dr Coughlan on regular occasions. Both of them were doing the crosswords, and Bishop Lucey asked Bishop Coughlan, 'well Dan, are you finished?'

'I'm not,' says Bishop Coughlan, 'I'm stuck, seven down and four across, they are looking for a four letter word, beginning with S and finishing with T, and 'tis a substitute for fertiliser.'

'That's quite simple,' replies Bishop Lucey, 'the word is soot.'

'That's right,' says Bishop Coughlan, 'pass me the rubber.'

I remember doing shows with him as a young lad in the Victoria Hospital for the patients. Dr Mary Ahern always welcomed us. As you can imagine the walls were covered with photographs and paintings of Queen Victoria and King George and many more English monarchs. When the concert was over we all sang our national anthem, *Amhrán na bhFiann,* and Hobbsie used mutter during the anthem, 'watch out for the photographs or they'll fall to the ground.'

Another memory of the wit of Dan is associated with a very famous wedding that took place in Cork many years ago. Thomas McCurtain, son of the famous Lord Mayor, married May Furey, who happened to be a neighbour of mine. Like many others, I went up to the Lough church to see the wedding. I can still see a beautiful bride and the stately figure of the groom as they walked down the aisle, out into the chapel yard under the guard of honour of the Cork Volunteer Pipe Band. When the band played 'Believe Me if All Those Endearing Young Charms' a few handkerchiefs appeared, a few sniffles could be heard.

I happened to be with Danny Hobbs who, like myself, witnessed all this splendour and style. As we strolled out the front gate a few women turned to Danny and said, 'you're leaving early, Dan!'

'I'm not,' says Hobbsie, 'I'm going home for the wife, to bring her up, because by what I saw today, we weren't married at all.'

I did a show in the Savoy Cinema with Dan Hobbs as compere. At that time there was no television or bingo, and any big name would fill the Savoy. The weekend of the show, the rumours were rampant around the city that Hobbsie had died. Even coming out of Mass on Sunday morning I had people asking me, 'come here Billa. Is it true Hobbsie kicked the bucket?'

The Savoy was packed that afternoon for the concert, and the audience waited with bated breath, to know would Hobbsie appear or not – well appear he did.

When the curtain went back, Hobbsie walked on to the Savoy stage with a white sheet covering his body, like a ghost, with Fred Bridgeman at the organ playing 'Danny Boy'. When Danny threw off the sheet and appeared in his striped suit and familiar dickie bow tie, there were roars of laughter and roars of relief.

The man was a rogue to the very end, a joy to know.

Of all my friends in the theatre world, and of all the acquaintances I ever encountered, to me the most loveable rogue of them all was Bob Carlisle. He was perfect for the part of Lord Fitzherbert in the *Up Cork* shows that ran in the AOH Hall for many years. He had this gentle grandeur, both on and off the stage. It made you smile and giggle in a very contented way, rather than release a hearty outburst of laughter. For example, where you and I would say, 'we'll go to Jackie Lennox for a chicken supper', Bob would say, 'let's call to Jackie's for a carcass'.

Or when we found ourselves up a mountain around Dingle, the hillside all ablaze with the burning of furze, he would say rather casually, 'regardless of the show, William, I do hope the natives are friendly.'

What a presence he created, when he walked on stage, dressed in county style, and wearing a grey moustache to go with his silver hair. He saved my bacon one night after an *Up Cork* show. I was damn glad of his presence. The show had been barely over when backstage came the principal girl and her father, gunning for me. She had been replaced that night just before the show. She had been looking for extra money, fifteen minutes before curtain and the crowd waiting. She was a lovely principal girl, and I feel now looking back, she had fallen in love with a young man of her own, and had enough of *Up Cork*. Her replacement had a blinder on the night; but the father of the regular principal girl read the riot act at me, as he tapped the hairs on my chest because I was still dressed in my stage attire.

'You're no man at all, Billa, to send my daughter home like you did. You think now, Billa, you're a great fella, with a car under your arse, but I remember a time down the Lough, when all ye had was a donkey.'

Bob tapped the father on the shoulder, and with his College Road accent said, 'donkeys, my good man, they were all the rage at the time.'

He defused the situation. He could judge the moment perfectly, as he did in St Patrick's Hall, Upton, another night. Most of the cast had travelled by bus, but Bob and a few more had travelled in my car. When we arrived, Fr Con Cottrell, the great Cork All-Ireland hurler – five medals he won – brought us in and produced a bottle of Paddy straight away. Bob had a good few. The rest of the cast arrived by bus and Seán Whyte, a great Cork actor in his day and fond of his little drop, got very annoyed because he had missed the bottle. What could I do? I had no answer. But then, as always, who arrived on the scene – none other than the Right Honourable Lord Fitzherbert himself, Bob Carlisle, who said, 'Seán, come here and I'll breath on you.'

All the tension lifted, just like the morning fog.

Even in a real crisis he still could deliver that gentle phrase. Consider the immortal line in a mini-bus crash, just outside Ballymacoda. We were all in a heap. Teresa Mc-Carthy, one of our Irish dancers, started saying her Act of Contrition: 'Oh my God, I am heartily sorry' when Bob turned to her, with his ear in his hand and said, 'enough of that my dear, let's get out of the wagon first.'

You couldn't beat Bob for that gentle, well-timed re-mark, even with his ear in his hand. Imagine, three nights later, with his ear stitched on, Bob was on stage performing in the Coliseum, Cobh. I could only conclude the man had nerves of steel. I thought he was incapable of losing his cool, until one windy night in Galbally, Co. Limerick when I witnessed an explosion. I heard Bob Carlisle, Lord Fitz-herbert himself, give expression to a view, about his fellow man that shocked me. It was who had said it, not what was said, that shocked me.

There we were next to each other, in a small dressing-room, getting ready for an *Up Cork* show. Bob was having slight difficulty with his grey moustache, when a tap on the window next to him broke his concentration, and a squeaky voice in a country accent said, 'excuse me sir, what time is the play starting?'

With typical cool cordiality, he turned to me and said, 'William, what time is curtain?'

'Half-eight,' I replied quickly.

Bob said out the window, 'curtain is at eight-thirty, eight-thirty.' And he recommenced securing his grey moustache, just beneath his nose.

Back came the squeaky voice again saying, 'excuse me sir, how much is the tariff?'

Bob raised his eyes to heaven, turned to me and said with a sigh, 'William, what is the admission?'

'Four and sixpence, and one shilling and sixpence,' I said.

Bob turned to our friend and repeated what I had said, when back again came the voice, this time squeakier than ever, saying, 'tell me sir, is the play good, is it worth a visit?'

'Twas like throwing a match on petrol. Bob exploded. 'get away ye miserable whore, you miserable misfortune, go away and see for yourself.'

The laughter came in through the window. Who was it, only Seán Whyte, a member of the cast. At last, we had found there was a limit to his patience. Such was the fun and innocent enjoyment we had, while on tour with *Up Cork* and other shows throughout the towns of Munster.

NO BIG HEADS IN CORK

Seán Whyte was a middle-sized man and very eloquent in speech. He was always ready with a fast line that would put you in your place very nicely if you were in danger of getting a swelled head.

I remember singing a duet with Bob Carlisle in the *Up Cork* shows – 'Darling I am Growing Old' and it used to stop the show every night. It was a wonderful feeling with the audience in the palm of our hands. We used to love singing it, but one night a woman started crying out loud, which made a member of the cast go down into the dressing-room to Seán.

'Come here, Seán,' he said, 'there's a woman in the third row, roarin' crying because of Billa and Bob.'

Seán Whyte looked at him and replied in his rich deep voice, 'no wonder she is, she wants her money back.'

I can assure you, there's no chance of a big head in Cork.

Another night in Skibbereen Town Hall, when we had finished *Up Cork,* I was being paid on the floor in front of the stage. Members of the Town Hall were stacking chairs, getting ready to close up. I had my bag with me, with the wig and make-up, Seán Whyte, ever helpful, started to walk down the hall, with a bit of scenery on one shoulder, and a pile of props on the other shoulder. I said to the fellow paying me, 'watch this now.'

Calling Whytie I said, 'Seán, will you take out my bag for me?'

He stopped and turned, loaded down as he was, and said, 'stick a brush in my mouth, and I'll brush the hall on the way out as well.'

As I said, he was very eloquent in speech, ever ready with the reply.

Another man of similar eloquence in speech, was Dick Deasy, the shoemaker, who had a beautiful baritone voice, and was a regular with Radio Éireann in the old Cork jail. His shoemaker's shop was next to the old Barrs Club, where Walls' bicycle shop is today. He was an excellent bootmaker, and when I worked with Thompsons I loved calling.

One day when I was handing in a pair of shoes a few customers were in the shop. For a ball-hop off Dick, I said in a pound-notish accent, 'I want these shoes soled and heeled, and would you please put leather on them this time, because the last time I'm sure it was cardboard. If you won't do as I ask, I'll take my business elsewhere.'

Dick, being a tall man, wearing glasses, looked out over them, studying me from head to toe. 'Do,' he said, 'take your business elsewhere, because when you came to me, I straightened your two legs for you, what God in heaven couldn't do for you.'

As I keep saying, you'll never get a big head in Cork.

When I recall Dick, I can see him with his black rim

around his mouth from the shoe nails. When my wife would go in to him he would be all over her, 'yes, my dear, no, my dear' wrapping her shoes in his fancy parcel with fancy twine, that read 'Richard Deasy – High Class Bootmaker'. But any time I went in to see him, parking my Thompsons van outside his shop, he would throw out the shoes on the counter at me, and bark, 'give me seven and six, and are you going to the match on Sunday?'

God rest him, a colourful character. We understood each other.

Equally colourful and one of the wittiest men I ever worked with was Christy Donovan, known to us all as 'Christy Props'. He worked all his years in the old Opera House and in the new Opera House. He was the man in charge of all the 'props' to be used on stage. He always wore a peak cap and was proud of the fact he was reared down the Coal Quay.

During *Summer Revels* or pantomime, Christy always went around with a box to all the dressing-rooms, to collect money for Lota. I shared a dressing-room with Paddy Comerford and when Christy came along with his box Paddy let on he was drained and exhausted after his television commercial that morning for B & I Ferries – all they used was his hands, handing in money at a cash desk!

'What's wrong with your man?' says Christy.

'Leave him alone,' says I, 'he's been on location all the morning.'

Christy turned to Paddy and said, ''twas a good job

you didn't do *The Ten Commandments.'*

That put Paddy in his place!

Another night Paddy and I were ready to go on stage as the ugly sisters in *Cinderella*. On the side of the stage Christy was having his usual banter with us. I turned and said, 'wouldn't you know your place, Christy. Don't you know all the great artists, before we go on stage, must get into character.'

Like lightning, Christy says, 'get away ye two chancers, ye couldn't get into Miahs.' The cheek of him!

Another time, during a dress-rehearsal for *Summer Revels* I was dressed as Madgie Murphy for a hospital sketch and, as ever, I had to get the costume checked by Pat Murray, our artistic director.

'It's too dark,' he says, 'go to Christy and get something bright or white for a contrast.'

Up I went to Christy Props in his corner where he had everything from a needle to an anchor.

'What's your problem?' says he.

I stood back and said, 'look at my costume, Pat Murray says it's too dark, and he's looking for something white or bright for the lapels of my jacket.'

'Wait now,' says Christy, 'I'll go up the Coal Quay and get ye a head of cauliflower.'

I recall another dress-rehearsal of *Cinderella* and all was not well. One magnificent scene is the ballroom scene, and the best artistic man in the country for creating this scene is Pat Murray. As theatre people know, he's acclaimed as the best in the business for all types of shows. He did a magnificent job with the ballroom scene. He had Cinderella's coach all lit up, and had ponies from Fossett's Circus pulling it. The costumes really made it a scene to remember. The highlight of the scene was just as Cinderella arrived in on the coach; Pat had arranged for stars to fall down from the flies – most effective, and got a round of applause every night.

The night of the dress-rehearsal we had the coach, Cinderella and the ponies, and the magnificent costumes – but someone had forgotten the stars. In shot Pat Murray from the auditorium, his artistic temperament in full flight, shouting, 'where are the stars, where are the stars?'

Quick as a flash, Paddy Comerford replies, 'we're here.'

Wouldn't you trust my good friend, Paddy – doesn't he have that way with words!

Paddy Coughlan of *Swans* fame was a very good comedian and very talented pianist. He had a brother Jack who was a very good pantomime baron. I remember him from my younger days in Fr O'Leary Hall. Jack Coughlan was a very witty and droll character. One night they went into the Glue-Pot in Glenbrook – a famous bar for a sing-along at the piano. A group of lads went down with Paddy and Jack expecting Paddy to play the piano while they were having a few pints. When they got into the pub there was another fellow playing the piano and he was so bad they tried in vain to get him off the stool. Then Jack Coughlan strolled

over and said, 'get up like a good boy, you're like a kanga-
roo dragging his pouch along the keys.'

THE INNOCENCE OF CHILDREN

The humour of children never fails to lift my heart, because it is never planned, never scripted. It simply rolls off the tongue, like the day my grandson, James, was in school attending a religious class. Fr Finbarr Crowley stood at the top of the class and was anxious to start the lesson so he asked a simple question. 'Well children,' he said, 'what special person was born on Christmas day?'

Now, as it happens I was born on Christmas day and without batting an eyelid, up shot my grandson's hand and says, 'my Granddad'.

I'm glad to say he is still in the school!

Another day, Mary, my eldest daughter, was bringing my granddaughter, Catherine, across London to Heathrow in the tube train. People in the carriage, complete strangers, started talking to Catherine. After a few minutes conversation, Catherine told them all, as proud as punch, 'anyway,' says she, 'my Granddad dresses up sometimes as a woman.' My daughter nearly died before the tube train made Heathrow.

My grandchildren are an audience all on their own, all seventeen of them; and every year the majority of them come together to see their Granddad in the pantomime in the Opera House. I remember one pantomime, a bedroom scene, and I was the Granny getting ready for bed. I finished up with a wig full of curling pins and my big platter face – 'the ball of the world' Paddy Comerford calls it – covered with vanishing cream. I had a face like Dracula. Then I had to walk down centre stage, out to the footlights and say to all the children, 'aren't I beautiful?'

A chorus of voices naturally shouted back, 'oh no you're not', to which I would reply, 'oh yes I am', and they would respond even louder 'oh no you're not'. But when the battle between myself and audience had died down, a little voice, which I recognised as one of my grandchildren, shouted up from the stalls, 'don't mind them Granddad, you're beautiful'. Make no mistake about it, blood is thicker than water!

Another night it was also a bedroom scene, but this time I had to get dressed behind the screen and eventually appear in one of those long night-dresses, down to my ankles, that our grannies wore so many years ago. I used to parade up and down the stage in my night-dress – written on the front in green block letters was 'Jack's Army'. Then I used to turn around and written on the back was 'here we go, here we go, here we go'.

Every night I used to ask the same question, 'do ye like me nightie?' and to tell the truth it always passed with flying colours. But this night, while I was boasting about my nightie to the children, a little girl came out of the third row of the front stalls and trotted up behind the orchestra pit. She shouted up at me, in her beautiful innocent voice, pointing to my nightie saying, 'anyway, my Mammy hasn't any.' The show stopped for a few minutes that night and, when the laughing died down, I spoke to the child and said,

151

'your mother will have your life when you go home.'

Still talking about pantomime bedroom scenes, for many years now I never go into bed as the granny without going down on my knees and saying my prayers, because of a lesson taught to me at a panto many years ago. I remember the show was *Aladdin* and I had the magic lamp in my bedroom. I hopped into bed, the lights when down on the stage, and I will always remember the lines to my dying day. I used say to the children 'nightie night!' And they would all answer back 'nightie night' and then I'd say, 'I love you' and all together the children would say, 'I love you'. This night I put my head on the pillow and a child's voice rang down from the circle saying 'Grannie, you never said your Hail Mary'. That child got a warm round of applause. The grannie got out of bed and apologised to the child, knelt down and said 'Hail Mary' – a lesson I never forgot!

And let me tell you something else about a night I was put in my place that I never forgot. I was one of the ugly sisters, during *Cinderella*, with Paddy Comerford. We were in the kitchen, giving poor Cinderella a terrible time. I was threatening her, telling her 'you are not going to the ball, you're not going to any ball. You make sure the hot water bottles are in the beds, and don't wake us too early in the morning, we need our beauty sleep.'

In desperation, a child came out from the third row, dashed up behind the orchestra, and shouted at me, 'let her alone, you fat fool.'

And let me tell you another story about the same scene in *Cinderella* on a different night. My grandson, James, was looking up at his Granddad giving out to Cinderella, shouting the same lines: 'you're not going to the ball. Have the hot water bottles in the beds, don't wake us in the morning.' Then we left the stage in our finery, with the boos from the children ringing in our ears. Along comes the Fairy Godmother, with her magic wand, and whisks Cinderella complete with coach, off to the ball to meet her prince. The music played up, the curtain came down, and the interval arrived.

James, my grandson, turns to his mum, saying, 'I must see my Granddad.'

'No, no,' replies his mother, 'you can't go backstage until the show is over.'

But he got so upset his mum decided to take him backstage to keep him happy. When he came into our dressing-room, I was surprised to see him during the interval. He said straight away, 'Granddad, I must see you, I have something to tell you.'

'What's your problem boy?' says I.

With that, he whispered into my ear, 'Granddad, I want to tell you, Cinderella is going to that ball.'

And I dared not doubt his sincerity. I looked at him, smiled, and said, 'thanks for marking my cards.'

When I think of that story I thank God for the magic of pantomime, and the innocence of children. I believe the magic and the innocence go hand in glove together. It is as important as learning to read and write. It is visual. They participate. They are all at play in their innocent minds. I can see the look of intensity in their faces. It is a wonderland up there upon that stage, and they are in it. Later on in life, when the magic has moved on, and the innocence all evaporated, the mind will reminisce, the magic will return, seen now through mature eyes, and happy feelings will emerge. Nostalgia has its place too within our hearts.

Why do parents love taking their children to pantomime? They bring them because part of the past is always alive within them. I accept many aspects of the past are best forgotten, but equally many aspects of our past, our innocent past, are best remembered. If and when a happy memory shoots across our minds, it should be arrested, and embraced for a little while, then let go free again, knowing it will return.

The joys of panto!

It's what comes out of a child, with that serious innocence, that I adore. No matter how absurd it may seem to us adults, we know the truth in all its simple logic has been spoken – and all we can do is laugh at it. A classic example of this kind of situation can be illustrated through a story told by Fr Vincent Daly, who used to tell it against himself, with great joy.

Fr Daly trained my second son, Chris, as an altar boy in the Lough church. When Chris joined the altar first he was only about eight years old. His first duty was 7.30 a.m. Mass during Lent. A senior altar boy was to be there with him, but he never turned up, which left Chris on his own with Fr Daly; Chris was very nervous as he walked around the sacristy. Fr Daly saw his predicament and tried to reassure him and told him not to worry. 'We'll get through this Chris boy, you and me together; we'll get through the job fine, don't worry.'

Just as they were going out the sacristy door to start the Mass, Chris turned to Fr Daly and said, 'Father, when you want me to ring the bell, do me a favour, just lift your left leg.'

And the nicest part of the story is Fr Daly actually did lift his left leg – during the offertory, up went the leg, the Consecration, up with the leg. It was all very simple logic to Chris. Potentially embarrassing to an adult, not to mind a priest, but he agreed with him and did it.

Isn't it true what they say, 'out of the mouth of babes!'

Take my son Bill, to this day he will reminisce about the *Wizard of Oz*. I played the cowardly lion, David McInerney was the Tin Man, and Paddy Comerford was the Scarecrow. The yellow brick road was a revolving one, and it was my son Bill, who was under the road, twisting the handle, as instructed by Tommy Burke, the stage manager. When reminiscing, Bill still boasts that he was the man who worked the yellow brick road. I hope when his little baby boy, Bill as well, grows up, he will have to listen to his father going on and on about the time he made the magic, and made the yellow brick road go round and round and round.

FIFTY YEARS OF PANTO

I am often asked where do I get the energy? How do I keep going? I don't know. I thank God. I keep going, it is as simple as that. But I do know the theatre is like gravity, the pull is there, applause is appreciation and it's nice. I would be a fool to deny that. There is a wonder and a magic in it all. You learn so much from the people you meet – my education had far more to do with the theatre than the classroom.

I sometimes wonder what my children and grandchildren think of me. At birthday parties when I would mention this imaginary character 'O'Grady', there was, and is, such excitement. O'Grady says hands up, hands down, touch your toes, left hand out, O'Grady says. You must do it because O'Grady says, and if you're wrong, you are out, you must obey O'Grady because O'Grady says. Then on another occasion I would conduct the dummy band. You do the action of the imaginary instrument you are given, but you can't laugh. Be the violinist or the drummer but don't laugh. I am the grand conductor; and move towards the table, climb on top, with an apple on a string, and snap-apple fun and frolics would all begin, with dumping in the water dish and water splashing all around the kitchen. My poor wife, Nell, pleading to take it easy, to mop it up, but to me it's panto time.

Alas time passes all so quickly. Children grow up and the grandchildren come along. To Farran Woods now we go, and play chasing in the woods with sticks for guns and trees to hide behind. Maybe I'll be around for the great-grandchildren. Can't you see me, climbing up upon my zimmerframe, shouting out O'Grady says? For some reason, and I don't know why, I get such happiness when I see children enjoying themselves. When I see children all excited and full of fun, I am on a high. I have difficulty with sadness. On one occasion as I drove my daughters Valerie, Judith and Mary to school, I noticed they looked sad and I returned home with them to Nell. I got the strangest look from Nell – a most unusual glance. Looking back I suppose it was a rather strange thing for a father to do, but at the time it made perfect sense to me.

In West Cork once, when we were about to go home after a month's holiday, Judith had fallen in love with Danny Cullinane's horse and she was crying her eyes out because she was leaving behind her beloved horse, Silver. Back I had to go, two miles in the lashing rain to Danny's farm, put a rug over Judith's head, so that she would not get a cold in the rain as she said goodbye again. Aren't I the eejit? But then such a memory can unexpectedly jump right into my mind in the strangest of places, and raise the heart, just like Valerie with Buttercup, the donkey, off buying carrots, or up on the cart with the churns and away we'd go to the creamery.

By contrast then, on another occasion I fell off the stage and broke some ribs during *Tops of the Town*. I got a painkiller injection into my ribs and went on that night. When my dear wife and faithful friend heard all this, I must admit, she was not amused. Looking back again it was a daft thing to do, but the reason why I'm saying it is that it does explain the gravity, the pull, the magic of a performance.

As a member of an audience, when the Barrs play the Glen, I feel the same thing, or when Cork play Tipperary; it must be a two-way tribal thing. Whatever it is, it has a life of its own, and the memories now are all stored away, with a strength all their own. They give me a secret confidence. I do not mean this in any egotistical way or in any way that would pump up my pride.

The same can be said about some famous people I have met along the way. Their simplicity and humility has always struck me as admirable. Tony Kenny is a man I loved working with and I was his mother in many a pantomime. When asked what kind of a fellow he is, my answer is always the same, 'he's the salt of the earth, one of our own.'

'I'm not surprised,' a woman replied on one occasion. 'He looks wholesome.'

Wholesome is the word, because one night when we had finished a dress-rehearsal around 1.30 a.m., he sat into his car as we were all heading for home.

'Are you heading back to Jury's, Tony?' I asked.

'No Billa, I'm going back to Dublin; my mother is not well.'

And do you know what – that man remembers me for all the mothering I gave him on stage. He told Mike Murphy in an interview they had one afternoon about wine, 'many is the bottle of wine I drank at different occasions, for different courses; but there's one course I'll always remember. If you ever want wine with skirts and kidneys go down to Billa's house in Cork.'

I'll never again boast about unique Cork dishes such as tripe and drisheen, and skirts and kidneys. My good wife Nell nearly beat me with the frying pan, when I told her who would be coming to have her skirts and kidneys, after a night's performance in the Opera House. Just as well divorce wasn't legal at the time, or I'd be sent off around the Lough. But do you know what she did? A very resourceful woman my wife is, despite the fact I was on cold pig for a week – she had a huge double stuffed pork-steak as a standby in case Tony Kenny, and Noel Ginnity (Noddy) who came along with him, didn't like the Cork dish. Not only did they enjoy the dish, but to this day when Nell and I meet Tony Kenny he always reminds us of that night in Cork, when we all sat down to have that famous Cork dish – those long thin skirts of pork, cut into chunks, boiled with a kidney and onion, seasoned with a beef cube and salt and pepper, and served with a chilled Chablis. Darina Allen eat your heart out!

But my dear Nell is quick to forget, which is just as well when I think of the night I had to calm her down in the bed in Rosscarbery. Mind you, what happened wouldn't exactly happen in the bedrooms around the Lough. Not that I'm going to explain all the things that actually happen in the bedrooms around the Lough. But what did take place in our bedroom in West Cork is quite normal for a rural setting. Nell had searched the whole of Rosscarbery for a few heads of cabbage, and a local character came up with the goods saying, 'I'll get ye cabbage for tomorrow's dinner, don't worry, I'll get ye cabbage'. But he didn't exactly tell us the time of delivery, and the manner in which he would deliver. At 3.00 a.m. in the morning, bang, crash on the bed. Roots, earth, stones and nettles and cabbage, the lot! Nell nearly took off, but I was there, cool, calm and collected, and if you believe that you'd believe anything – but the curly green was beautiful, as wholesome as Tony Kenny himself was!

As I'm talking about Dublin people I had the pleasure of meeting Gay Byrne, a very nice, warm and friendly fellow, a very professional man. At the Carling Talent Contest Gay Byrne had such an eye for detail, he was a perfectionist and as chairman of the adjudicating panel, before the curtain went up, he was the only one to ask me what chair he would be sitting on. He commanded fierce respect.

It was out of that contest the all-Cork *Late Late Show* of April 1982 was born. More precisely, it was the Beamish hospitality room where we used to have a party after the Carling Contest in the Opera House. Gay Byrne was so impressed with the carry-on he said, 'I must bring this talent up for the *Late Late Show*.'

That's where I saw the true professional at work. The preparation he put in, to make it all look so relaxed as if unplanned. Not to mind the power of television – Paddy

Comerford and myself were national heroes – we got such recognition the following day.

In a crowded lift going down to breakfast a woman said, 'aren't ye the two boys on the *Late Late Show* last night?'

And there was I struggling with the bags. We were never used to this fame. Typical Comerford of course, when the lift opened at the ground floor, he turned to me and said, 'Billa, leave the bags as they are, call the porter and we'll live it up.'

It was the same at breakfast, or at a petrol station or a restaurant down the country for coffee: 'There's the man who told the story about the pigeons.'

They were kissing Paddy and hugging him and shaking his hand. Eventually he came over to us, and captured the mood of the entire experience in typical Paddy fashion when he said, 'do you know what Billa, I think we'll walk from Fermoy.'

We enjoyed the fame, knowing next week would be another show, and short-lived fame for somebody else, but I must also say not realising you might be recognised can be embarrassing too, very embarrassing come to think of it.

I was in the Gran Canaries in Playa-del-Ingles and the place was full of Germans. I found them very aggressive, grabbing chairs around the pool, walking past you as if you didn't exist, you know the type. We went on a day trip out to Puerto Rico, with me in my shorts, shining, soaked in sun oil and my good wife Nell equally dressed in shorts and top as well. I saw this big heavy blonde woman staring at us. Every time I would throw a glance she would be staring.

'Look at that big German blonde woman over there, she can't stop gaping at us,' I said.

Then I put my arm around Nell's waist. 'Come on,' says I, 'and we'll give that big German blonde something to talk about.'

Then as I passed her, I said in broken English, 'we honeymoon couple, honeymoon couple we.'

'I wouldn't doubt you, Billa. Is it there you are?'

The woman was from Bishopstown.

We slipped away quietly after the briefest of chats. You don't really recover from these situations at all. I know when the game is lost. Recognition has its downside as well, but once you know it is only a passing feeling, the feet never leave the ground. As some poet said 'The paths of glory lead but to the grave'. Not that I was one for deep poetry, but the odd line from schooldays has stuck, and thankfully as they say in Kerry, 'you'd never lose the run of yourself.'

When I was much younger attending the Cork Film Festival in the 1960s I had the pleasure of meeting film stars of world fame, like Trevor Howard, Jack Palance and James Mason, and well-known Irish artists too, like Noel Purcell and Cecil Sheridan. Patrick's Street and all around the Savoy used be jammed with crowds pushing and shoving to see their favourite stars.

As a sales rep with Beamishs I had to attend the Film

Festival most nights and the Festival Club in the City Hall afterwards. As I sat at a table on my own one night who approached me saying, 'I believe you do a lot of variety shows in Cork' – the one and only James Mason. As we sat and chatted away, I was struck by his unassuming manner despite his world fame. There was no need for me to lose the run of myself for the rest of my career on stage. I can't recall much of the chat I had with Jack Palance because as he spoke I could only see the gunslinger in the western film *Shane* in front of me. His simplicity was charming. I didn't expect it out of a gunslinger, which shows you what images in your head could do.

One of the most vivid memories I have of the Film Festival is the actress Dawn Adams and her milk bath. She was a low-sized lady, dark haired, very attractive; the kind of lady who loved showing off all her condition. When she stayed in the Metropole Hotel she demanded a milk bath as a publicity stunt. Douglas Vance, the manager, very popular and highly respected, refused point-blank, but the story leaked to the press and it was the biggest ball-hop in Cork for weeks after.

Did you hear about the woman who fell into a lot of money? She went up and asked Douglas Vance for a milk bath. He called the staff and organised it at once for the woman, one of our own. There she was in the bath, dressed in her altogether, when a porter, trying to be smart, says, 'well Mrs, do you want it past-ur-eyes?'

"Ere, no boy,' says she, 'up as far as me arse will do me.'

Isn't it amazing how memories flood back when you sit back, relax and review the past with pride? Have I regrets? Not one. The instinct to survive is there since early childhood. I'm meeting targets all my life, not just targets for sales of Beamish, but rather security for my family, not just financial security, but security in love as well. That they would feel it, and the grandchildren now too would feel it, despite my cranky moments, despite the flash that comes from a fuse sometimes on the short side. Family loyalty has driven me, and in good faith I have responded. When I meet my maker it will matter little who knew me or how many famous people I met along the way, but I hope He will say to me, 'you made a lot of people happy, Billa, well done.'

The memory now of my son Bill and daughter Carol-Ann, happy – playing golf with hurleys, digging holes in the shifting sand – is as important as me playing in the Emerald Ballroom, Shepherd's Bush, with Dickie Rock and his Echoes, and Val Doonican, long before they became household names; or playing Grand Marshal for the St Patrick's Day Parade, beside the Lord Mayor, Dave McCarthy, a prominent member of St Vincent's Hurling and Football Club, and the City Councillors dressed up in official robes. A little young fellow caught my eye as, proud as a peacock, he was passing by on the St Vincent's Hurling Club float, all dressed up in St Vincent's colours, green jersey and white knicks. He shouted up to our Lord Mayor, 'I wouldn't doubt you, Davey boy.'

'I'll give you, Davey,' replied the Lord Mayor, waving

his fist and smiling with good-humoured.

'That wouldn't happen anywhere else in the world,' says Jack Higgins, the City Manager, sitting beside me, 'and long may it last,' he added.

I know what he means, because what Bishop Buckley said to me had that same touch. When he was installed at the cathedral, a nun at Turner's Cross phoned me to tell me that the bishop had left a ticket for a seat in the cathedral, and the bishop said 'that 'tis happening on a Sunday and that you, Billa, might be going to a match.'

Talk about knowing your flock. Again that same loveable bishop couldn't come to a function for Monsignor O'Callaghan in the Munster Arms, Bandon, due to rehearsals for Holy Week. A young curate came in to me before the show – and I a bag of nerves – and said, 'Billa, the bishop was just on the telephone saying he can't make the function tonight because of rehearsals for Holy Week. Would you explain to the people how he was held up, and he also said to tell Billa if there is any other change in the diocese I will let him know.' Surely the little boy from St Vincent's Club and myself, have proven that the gap between 'officialdom' and the 'ordinary' is very small in Cork.

All of this is a long way from Cois na Páisté in Ballingeary as a boy, where Brendan Breen, known as Mac Uí Breen must have spotted something in me. There was a show being put on in Ballingeary when we were out in Doire na Birce, three miles away, and out of all the hundreds of young lads he asked John Foley and me would we like to

165

see the show. Years after as a rep with Beamishs, I met him in Mount Mellary where he ended his days teaching, and I asked him why did he pick me.

'I knew the day would come, Billa, when you would tread the boards with style.'

Without encouragement at a tender age, how different things might have been! When you realise somebody believes in you it is very good for your own self-belief, because there are times when you feel used, which always upsets me. I find it hard to say no, but I want to survive. What do you think of this fellow I met going down Whyte Street – 'Hello, Billa, the right man in the right place. Do a job for me tonight?'

'Forget it, if you didn't see me, you wouldn't want me.'

He was stunned, but give me a break!

On another occasion I had finished a six-week run in the Opera House. I had given it my all. I was drained. I flew out to Portugal and when Nell and I landed, the crowd from Cork wanted me to go out with them. I explained and explained and eventually said no. She walked back to her group and I heard another woman say, 'you're worse to ask him. I told ye, he's a pain in the arse.'

It really upset me and when that nasty memory pops up from nowhere in my mind, I compensate by thinking of the night I was invited over to London, to the Wembley Conference Centre, where I did my act to an all-Irish audience, with an all-Irish cast and three and a half thousand people staring up at me. They all laughed and clapped and made me feel good. Good memories cancel out the bad. That's life I suppose.

One final memory that stands out as the proudest moment of my entire career – this memory I cherish above them all. Nell and I went to Lourdes with the Cork and Ross Diocese with Monsignor Hayes and Fr Michael McCarthy from Bantry as our spiritual directors. Monsignor Hayes came into the hotel where we were staying and said, 'Billa, I'm saying Mass at the Grotto in the morning, would you sing the Mass?'

I declined straight away. 'Father, I'm not Pavarotti at all you know.'

'Billa boy,' he said, 'I don't want you to sing solo at all, only lead the hymns.'

I agreed. I did not get a wink of sleep that night. This was a whole new experience for me. No jokes, no jumping or prancing about on a pantomime stage. I couldn't stop thinking of the great occasion. When the dawn broke and the morning sun peeped above the rim of the world, 'twas like the curtain going up on a brand new stage for me. When the time came, down I went early, on my own, beside the grotto. The peace and silence, and the balmy breeze blowing up along the river, calmed me.

The people in wheelchairs came with all their helpers; the others followed with all their banners raised. Just before the priests arrived, I went over under the statue of Our Lady and I prayed like I never prayed before, to have her see me right on this big occasion. As I prayed I noticed a big chestnut in the crack of the rock beside me, and what do you think I did, I put out my hand, took the chestnut and put it in my pocket. Why, I'll never know, but I still have it. Then up I stood, gazed across the congregation, saw all the banners from all over Ireland out in front, and many others further back and slowly started into the opening hymn. The people joined in, and in a few minutes it all sounded like one big huge choir. By the time I got to 'Faith of our Fathers, in spite of dungeons, fire and sword' I was ready for canonisation.

I lived off the moment for days on end, and couldn't stop talking about it to Nell. I was wound up; but I must say, least anybody think I had some kind of apparition or heavenly stroll, that I came down to earth with a bang on a subsequent trip to Lourdes, while on a bus up to Bartres. We sat on the back seat with Brian Barrett, chairman of the County Board, and his wife. A sing-song started. I felt sure nobody knew me. I kept my head down, but unknown to me, there were two women from Cork up in the front row of the bus. In a short while I head the courier request over the microphone in broken, pidgin English, 'vill Billa come to sing song please, please Billa to sing song.'

Up I went, did my party piece as they say, and on my way back to my seat, a woman from up the country with a fine Irish brogue, tapped me on the shoulder and said, 'God, you're great altogether, you should be on the stage.'

'Thank you, ma'am,' said I, and sat down.

There you have it, life, and its ups and downs. Time

passes, and it seems to pass more quickly as I get older. The theatre has been good to me, and when I see others happy as I do my act on stage, it means the world to me.

Titbits

I always say Cork humour can be vicious and wicked. I remember standing at a bar one day, when I working for Beamishs. Two fellows came in and decided to have two pints and one fellow said to the other under his breath, 'make sure you go to the husband for the pints, because his wife couldn't fill a half one.'

Fear ag Obair

Coming in from West Cork, having done a show of a winter's night, I was coming down by Spur Cross and drove into a flood. Before I knew it, I was up to my ankles in water. I left the car there and started walking with my shoes squelching, feeling cold and miserable, in the middle of nowhere, three o'clock in the morning.

I had walked a mile along this back road, when I saw a car backed into a laneway, and as they say in West Cork, 'do bhí an fear ag obair.' When I knocked at the window, the boy and girl nearly passed out with fright.

'Ould stock,' says I, 'my car is on the side of the ditch, all flooded. Would you ever give me a spin, I'm only a few miles from home?'

As he drove along, with me in the back seat, he kept on saying, 'don't ever mention this off the stage, or I'll never forgive you.'

That night I didn't know who the boy and girl were.

Their secret will be buried with me, because I still don't know who they are!

Mass-card Annie

Mass-card Annie was a character Paddy Comerford knew in the northside many years ago. God love her, during her lifetime one of her legs had to be amputated. Annie insisted the leg should be buried in the family plot in the Curraghcapawn graveyard, which is nearly half-way out to Blarney. While she was alive, every Christmas she would make the journey up to the Curraghcapawn and place a sprig of holly on the grave.

Doesn't it take all kinds to make a world, and what people do never ceases to amaze me.

Owenahincha

Paddy Connolly used to own the hotel in Owenahincha. One night as Paddy was standing at his pub door, a busload of Americans arrived at around eleven o'clock at night, and weren't too sure if they would be served or not. One Yank asked Paddy, 'what time do you close, sir?'

Paddy turned and said, 'October, sir.'

Jack Doyle and Christy Ring

Some say Jack Doyle captures all that is wild and wonderful in us Irish, and at the same time captures all that is gentle and sensitive as well. He was definitely one of the most loveable and colourful characters I ever met and he ordered me to fix a meeting with the maestro himself, Christy Ring. In Jack's head, Christy was the ultimate hero.

I could have got a photograph of Christy and Jack Doyle having coffee together, smiling and laughing. I thought the cup of coffee would only be a half-hour or an hour at most but they enjoyed each others company so much it went on for hours. Every night after that when Jack Doyle came on stage he would tell his audience, 'I met Christy Ring.'

Two legends, the Gorgeous Gael and Cuchulainn himself – what a picture, what a photograph – but I never snapped it!

Hard to imagine poor Jack died alone and broke in St Mary's Hospital in Paddington, London. He earned as much per week as Roy Keane is earning today. He socialised with the likes of Clarke Gable and Errol Flynn and was adored by women, married a Mexican beauty, actress Movita. She divorced him and married Marlon Brando.

Both Jack and Christy had a lot in common – they could excite a crowd, create an electric atmosphere, one with his voice and the other with a flick of a wrist or a solo run for goal. That quality to create magic fascinates me. When Jack would sing 'Mother Machree' or 'The Rose of Tralee' he would have them all in the palm of his hand. Likewise with Christy, when he got possession of the ball the crowd would get hysterical, as they knew something special was going to happen. Christy's will to win was frightening. He played squash in later life with that same will to win. I suppose it contributed to his heart attack when he collapsed outside the College of Commerce.

Two wonderful people – God rest them both.

Jackie Healy-Rea

I love meeting Jackie – a larger than life character, with a turn of phrase all his own. Seán Ó Sé, a great friend of Jackie's, was doing a show one night for him below in his Lounge Bar in Kilgarvan. The Lounge Bar was packed and, after a few songs, Seán felt he wasn't being heard at all. He went to Jackie and asked him to turn up the amplification and the answer he got was, 'you're sound out, Seán boy, because if it's any louder, you'll be only making a nuisance of yourself.'

Wasn't that encouraging!

Jackie Lennox

I have never got over this one, I'll have to take it to the grave. Jackie must be the most famous chipper in the country. Not only did I know Jackie well, but I knew his mother and father – they were great theatre people.

One year when all our children were very small, I invited Jack and family to Rosscarbery for a day. They arrived on a Friday, the time of the black fast, when no meat at all was allowed on a Friday. I was sent scouring Rosscarbery for fish all to no avail, not a kipper to be had. As you know, Jackie and his family work with chips fifty weeks of the year and he came down to Nell and myself to get away from it all. But as he sat down with us to have a meal, we

173

could only give him a meal of chips, beans and eggs! God rest Jackie, he never let me forget it. He used to say, 'Billa, I work all day every day, cutting chips, and frying chips and putting chips into bags and parcels and end up below in Rosscarbery eating chips with you!'

Many is the laugh both of us would have when he would see me standing in the queue for my chicken supper. He never let me live it down!

My First Radio Microphone

Etna Dunne, the blonde bombshell, brought the microphone down from Dublin with her, to appear in the Country Club. It was the size of a long thick black pudding, with a lead hanging out of it and it was a very sensitive microphone. When I introduced the Bombshell I handed her the microphone. Just as she was about to sing, a taxi passed the Country Club, and we could all hear quite clearly through the microphone, a voice asking the driver, 'would Cab 17 pick up a fare at the Bus Office, Parnell Place.'

With the Cork accent, she knew well that she was in Cork!

At the Ballet

Finbarr Ronayne's grandson is a big fan of mine and he never misses the pantomimes, but off he went on this occasion to the ballet with his Granddad. The crowd in the Opera House were sitting in silence, a very appreciative audience, enraptured by the dancers on stage. In the middle of the silence a shout rings out from the circle, 'Granddad, when is Billa coming on?'

He had seen the pantomime the week before. Can you imagine me, strutting on stage, handbag and wig, doing a *pas-de-deux* with Paddy Comerford?

Kevin O'Leary

My relationship with cars is a bit unusual. If I get a puncture I would want to nearly sell the car. When I open the bonnet, I could scream when I see all the wires and plugs and chambers and tubes, and combustion here and combustion there. How could any brain put all that together, and make it move!

Kevin O'Leary, the motor-car man himself, showed me a measure of kindness I thought had disappeared since the arrival of the Celtic tiger. It was indeed above and beyond the call of duty. My car stopped dead outside Bandon GAA pitch one afternoon. I had a show that night in Limerick and another show the following night and here I was on the roadside – panic and perspiration pouring out of me. I pushed it, with help, into the nearby petrol station owned by Kevin O'Leary.

'I can't do anything for you,' said the petrol boy, 'but I'll make a phone call.'

Along comes Kevin O'Leary himself in his own car. 'Sit in,' he said. He drove me to the other side of Bandon, where he has his showrooms. He opened up, took out a new car, and said, 'There you are, Billa, off you go to Limerick.'

Not many would do that. No wonder he is a successful businessman.

Mick Barry, Up Cork *and the Viaduct*

Many years ago there was a bowl contest, at the Viaduct sponsored by Dunlops, to see who would be the first man to loft the Viaduct. If my memory serves me right, Mick Barry was the only man to put a 16 oz. bowl on top of the Viaduct. The *Up Cork* show was on at the time and we had a sketch in which I, as Madgie Murphy, would loft the Viaduct. I was being shown road by Paddy Cotter. It was a hilarious part of the show. Instead of a bowl I had a black hard handball which I used throw every night into the wings, doing harm to no one.

This night, unfortunately, the ball or the bowl hit my knee, bounced on the stage and landed on a woman's lap in the front row. The poor misfortunate woman nearly lost her reason. She really thought a bowl had struck her.

Fr Mathew Hall and Cinderella

I remember one *Cinderella* in Fr Mathew Hall when I played the ugly sister opposite Ned Collins, a great character with a very soft and gentle voice. We had no microphones in pantomime at the time. The show was on a few nights and a very tall, serious-looking man, Fr Mathew, the spiritual director of Fr Mathew Hall, came into our dressing-room. He looked at Ned and said, 'my good man, would you speak up during the show, the people in the third row are anxious to hear you.'

Good Thinking

Dick Deasy was a bootmaker in Barrack Street. One night he was in a pub downtown – when to be caught after hours was a mortal sin. Dick was having his few pints in the flat of the city when they heard a rat-tat on the door, and a deep voice bellowed out 'guards on duty'.

Customers scattered up stairs and down stairs. Dick, being the sound man that he was, went to the front door, took off his coat before he opened the door as if he was a member of the staff, and said, 'come in guard.'

In they came. Dick put on his coat, walked out the door into the darkness of the night, scot-free!

The Fox and Hounds and the Tape

A pub I enjoyed calling to during my time in Beamishs was Mick and Elsie's Fox and Hounds in Ballyvolane. When I made my tape called *Billa* I was thrilled when Elsie informed me one day over my usual coffee, 'Billa,' says she, 'I play your tape every night.'

'I'm delighted to hear that Elsie, it goes to show you are a woman of good taste.'

'I have it on all right, but I also make sure 'tis closing time!'

The Power of the Cloth

Fr Doody was a great friend of mine for many years and a regular to all our shows in the city. I was led to believe that if he had not been a priest he would have made it big in the theatre as a Shakespearean actor. He was a tall, dark man, with a very rich voice. He went from being curate in St Peter and Paul's to parish priest in Schull. He invited me to bring a concert party to Schull and I remember well the letter he wrote me. It started like this: 'My dear Billa, You must come to Schull, it's now at its loveliest.'

We fixed the date, a Sunday night in August. We set off to Schull, John R. O'Shea, myself and a few of the lads. When we arrived in the hall, which was packed, the lads as usual went for a few pints before the show. At about 8.30 p.m., I was the only one backstage, when who arrived but the bold Fr Doody, saying, 'well Billa, are we ready to start?'

'Father,' says I, ''tis only half-past eight.'

'It is down to start at half-eight and start we will,' came the reply.

I then told him the lads were gone to the pub, a few doors up from the hall, for a few jars. Out he walked, stood at the pub door and shouted, 'city artists, out!'

And they walked out like young schoolboys from a class. Those were the days!

Guide Dogs

One day as I was collecting for the Guide Dogs, a shopkeeper called me, and told me an elderly lady had left an envelope for me with a donation for the Guide Dogs. I asked the shopkeeper for her name but she wanted to remain anonymous. When I opened the envelope, the donation amounted to £200 in cash, with a lovely note, clipped on to the money saying, 'For the Blind Dogs'.

A Confused Consultant

Peter Sheriff, a consultant from England, visited Beamishs regularly. The first day he arrived I was asked to show him around the city-centre pubs and as we were driving out through the brewery gate, I turned and said, 'I hope you won't find the Cork accent too fast to pick up.'

He looked at me and said, 'I beg your pardon.'

New Year in Redbarn

I worked a lot for the Luceys – Murt, Gerry and Michael – who owned the Majorca in Crosshaven, and Redbarn in Youghal. I remember bringing in the New Year in Redbarn with Donal Kenneally, and I had got a loan of a Third Order habit from the Holy Trinity. Gerry Lucey had a scythe waiting for Old Father Time. I was on the stage seeing out the old year, telling the people to let their troubles go out with the tide, and to see Old Father Time out of the hall as the people made a pathway for him down the centre of the hall. Here I was on stage, wishing everybody peace and goodwill for the New Year, but just as Donal Kenneally got to the bottom of the hall, some smart alec decided to give him a kick up the arse. If he did, Kenneally gave him a swipe of the scythe and there I was, singing 'Auld Lang Syne' with the New Year in, and Old Father Time still in the back of the hall flaking the lard out of some local smart ass.

Tony Kenny

In a production of *Cinderella* Tony Kenny played Prince Charming. One night, as the ugly sister, while I was trying to play up to him, I called him Tony instead of Prince Charming and the audience erupted when they discovered my mistake. It went so well, we decided to let it in. When I met people afterwards they were all praise for the show, and the most natural question I would ask was, 'what night were you in?' The answer I got sometimes was, 'it was in the night you called Prince Charming Tony.'

And God forgive me, I never had the heart to tell them!

Jim Reeves

Redbarn was a very popular dance hall in Youghal, Co. Cork during the 1960s. It was particularly popular during the summer time because it was beside the sea, the sandy dunes and the wide open strand stretch all the way to Youghal town itself.

For Gerry Lucey, the night that Jim Reeves appeared was very special because when Jim had finished his spot on stage he went for a walk along the beach with Gerry as it was a beautiful summer's evening. Naturally, Gerry felt good strolling along beside such a marvellous singer, who enjoyed world fame at the time. One of his greatest hits had been, 'Put Your Sweet Lips a Little Closer to the Phone'. There he was on this August night, with a balmy breeze blowing in from the sea, a glorious harvest moon hanging over Youghal bay, glistening on the waves as they rolled to the shore. There and then Jim Reeves stopped and listened, and in a little while he broke into song, singing 'Red Sails in the Sunset'.

That's still vivid in my head, as if I had been there, as if it all happened to me. What intrigues me is when my mind wanders, and goes off on a voyage, my imagination can visualise a happy experience I may have had, or a friend like Gerry Lucey may have shared with me. It makes me feel the wonder and see the beauty.

A lifetime in the theatre can help tremendously to keep the imagination alive. I know exactly where Jim Reeves was coming from, and how it captivated Gerry Lucey. I sometimes feel I have had about three lives packed into one – all the variety shows, the pantomimes, etc., but for me it is the stage that keeps the imagination vivid, and up-beat. An interest in live theatre can explode the imagination into a wonderland, full of pleasant experiences that can lift our hearts to the very stars above. The real beauty about 'Red Sails in the Sunset' is that Jim Reeves, the performer, captured the moment because of his imagination, and Gerry Lucey, his audience, recognised it. Both were happy ever after.

In Court

I was summoned to appear in the Cork District Court, long before the traffic wardens existed, for illegal parking. When I arrived at the court for 10.00 a.m., there was a great friend of Seán Ó Sé's, District Justice Len Clifford, a man I had met many times with Seán through Gael-Linn.

Our cars at the time in the brewery were leased from Kevin O'Leary, on the back Douglas Road, under the title Leeside Leasing. By some strange coincidence the clerk called out a traffic summons from somebody with an address at Beamish & Crawford Brewery, Cork. It was not me.

I sat there, waiting for someone to show up from Beamish & Crawford, but no one did. District Justice Clifford got a great laugh from the courthouse chamber when he bellowed down from the bench, 'well, Mr O'Connell, are you going to sit there and be silent for a change?'

Lent Long Ago

I did shows for Canon Roberts of Christchurch, right beside where Bishop Lucey Park is now. They had an annual event, and I've lovely memories of Canon Roberts, a tall grey-haired man, always riding a bicycle.

One year they held their event during Lent and I was asked to entertain and also asked to join the gathering afterwards for a meal. As I sat at the table and saw this magnificent spread in front of me, my conscience must have troubled me, because while I'm a good man at the table, I was inclined to hold back because of the season of Lent.

Canon Roberts saw my dilemma, leant across and whispered in my ear, 'Billa, eat away boy, I'll give you a special dispensation, you're in a different parish tonight.'

Ger Howe

Ger Howe worked in the Gas Company. He was a great Glen Rovers man and became president of Sullivan's Quay past pupils union in the south side. His job was collecting money from gas meters and over he went, up Blarney Street with a bag of coppers thrown over his shoulder. He knocked on the door of a house, opened by a woman who screamed, 'the mouse, the mouse!'

'Don't worry Mam,' says Ger, 'I'll fix him.'

He swung his bag of coppers and spattered the mouse off the skirting board and wall. It was her pet mouse and she was only afraid he would run out on the road.

Diver Casey

Diver was a well-known Cork character, GAA and rugby fan. His favourite song was 'Beautiful City'. The morning of his funeral Mass in Togher church, I was asked by the family would I sing 'Beautiful City'. I knew him so well I couldn't refuse.

I cleared everything with the priest in Togher, and sang 'Beautiful City' backed by the Friendship Singers as the coffin went down the aisle. There wasn't a single dry eye in the church. Outside in the churchyard, many people came up to me, to compliment me, saying, 'Billa, that was beautiful.'

But it must be said, often in life close to tears there is laughter. Next up to me came this fellow with a glint in his eye, saying, 'you really did justice to Diver and "Beautiful City".' Then with a twinkle in his eye, tongue in cheek, he says, 'when I go, Billa, put me down for "Are you right there Michael, are you right".'

Bishop Casey and the Examiner

A relation of Bishop Casey died in the Lough Parish some years ago. The evening before the funeral Mass, a journalist from the *Examiner* rang Canon William Shinkwin, parish priest of the Lough: 'Tell me, canon, is it true that Bishop Casey is arriving in Cork airport in the morning?'

'You're right,' says the canon.

'Tell me,' says the journalist, 'is he saying the funeral Mass for his relation?'

'Right again,' says the canon.

'One more question,' says the journalist, 'is the Mass at ten o'clock in the morning?'

'You're spot on,' says the canon.

'Would you mind telling me, canon,' said the journalist, 'where did you get your information?'

The canon simply replied, 'I read it in tonight's *Evening Echo*.'

Rosscarbery

Over a few pints one night, I inquired from one of the locals in my innocence, about a woman who was always looking out her window every time I passed. No matter what time I passed there she'd be, peeping out behind the curtains.

I asked the local what was the situation regarding her always looking out. 'That one,' says he, 'she's like a light-house.'

Saint Francis

When the present St Francis church was being built, and while the friars were demolishing the old church, most Corkonians will recall a big railing around the old church and churchyard. A lovely Cork story comes out of the whole affair – about two Cork women, complete with black shawls, who were complaining about the Franciscans knocking the old church and building the new.

'Ah,' says one as the rain bate down on both of them, 'them priests have short memories, look at St Francis, and the rain hopping off him; without a cape or a canopy over him; oh dey have short memories.'

'You're right,' says her buttie, 'look where we used to kneel, and got what we wanted, and 'tis now covered with weeds and nettles, you're right, dem priests have short memories all right.'

As they said their goodbyes, one stuck her head right up to the railing, and shouted, 'St Francis, I hope you're in Heaven anyway boy.'

Ireland 2; Spain 1
Manager: Bill O'Connell
Venue: South of Spain, Torremolinos
Ireland: European Champions

Five-a-side soccer on an all-weather pitch. I witnessed tremendous passion. Twelve months later I was out there again, sitting by the pool, learning my script for *Summer Revels*. I spotted Eddie Halloran of Cobh Ramblers talking to George Meldrick. My own son, Bill and Dave Barry were there as well as Nell, and Seán Hayes of Nemo Rangers.

While I was never good at sums I thought of the five-a-side and all the excitement of last year, straight away I went to the receptionist and entered Ireland for the competition, managed by Bill O'Connell of St Finbarrs and Cork.

Mick McCarthy step aside I said, with all this defensive stuff playing away from home, and big Jack with the big long ball, catch them on the turn, not a chance. We were playing in temperatures no man should be allowed walk around in, not to mind play football in; and yet I had to keep my squad focused; national pride was at stake, you know yourself, scratch me and I'm green all over – aren't we all!

There were the English prancing around the place, all mouth, thinking they were all 'Gazzas'; and the Germans deadly serious, going through some kind of drill, ready to go to war. You had the French and the Italians, the Belgians, the Danes – they were all there.

'Right lads,' says I, 'I'm announcing my squad. In goal and sweeper, Seán Hayes of Nemo Rangers, my two defenders are Eddie Halloran of Cobh Ramblers and Bill O'Connell of St Finbarrs. My two strikers are George Meldrick of Cobh Ramblers and Dave Barry of the Barrs and Cork' – and he's the present-day manager of Cork City!

Dave Barry said he was on his honeymoon, which he was, but it was not accepted as a possible excuse for a poor performance. His country came first; and the heat out there in that pitch was not to be compared with honeymoon heat. I had to keep a special eye on him, so that he wouldn't lose his concentration, or be sparing energy for another game elsewhere. Discipline was vital because the Spaniards were very cocky. They had won this competition many times and were practically unbeatable. They were the pick of the staff from the complex, playing together year after year.

People came off their sunbeds in droves to see this socalled Irish wonder team. There was bottles of water and perspiration, dehydration and inspiration hanging in the heat of the Spanish sun. Spain are still trying to work out what happened – where did this Irish team come from, where did they get all this talent, all the fancy first touches, little flicks, back heel nudges and handy headers.

It was serious stuff and don't think for a moment there was nothing at stake, even though it was only a box of champagne we raised aloft when victory finally came our way. It was our hearts and our pride that went pop that night, not the corks. Still we all got together like true Europeans. We sat and sipped, and watched the sun fall away below 'the world' until it disappeared; and left the sea all covered in a rich red glow.

No wonder Dave Barry says to me any time we meet, 'Billa, you were the wisest manager of all time. You knew when to pull out, at the top.'

Epilogue

Another very proud moment for Billa, and his family, was the day he opened a letter from the National University of Ireland, asking him would he like to accept an Honorary MA for his lifetime's contribution to the theatre in Cork. Surely such a moment, with such a letter in anyone's hand, would make anyone say it is time to sit back, relax, and review the past with pride. But knowing Billa, and that very strong sense of family he has, he would feel the honour conferred upon him by University College, Cork, more for his family, and his friends in the theatre, than ever he would feel it for himself. Such is the man.

Naturally, he was delighted to accept this prestigious award; and as it happened, by a happy co-incidence, his son Chris was also conferred with a BA on the very same day, 26 July 1996.

Then, to crown it all, another great honour was given to him by the Lord Mayor, Councillor Joe O'Flynn, in April 1999. On behalf of the people of Cork, a Civic Reception was extended to him, for his fifty years in the theatre.

It really was making official that wonderful warm feeling this man creates in the hearts of all Corkonians; and was it not only right and fitting! That same feeling was captured in a gesture by a taxi-driver as he drove Billa and his wife to the City Hall. The taxi-driver saw Billa was dressed in his Sunday best. 'Billa boy,' he says, 'where are you off to?'

'Believe it or not,' replies Billa, 'I'm getting a Civic Reception in the City Hall.'

They drove along, and when they got to the City Hall, naturally Billa asked, 'how much do I owe you?'

The taxi-driver's reply said it all, for all of us, when he said, 'Billa, for all the laughs, and all the enjoyment you gave to us, young and old, year after year, this one is on me, boy.'

GLOSSARY

Ball-hop = innocent fun, comment that would provoke another person

Barrs = short name for St Finbarr's Hurling and Football club

Being shown road = shown where to throw the bowl

Boga = outside toilet

Dá flaitheas Dé = God in Heaven

Divers tongues = prone to a little bad language

Donkey's gudge = cake

Fair Hill drag hunt = a sporting event in Cork – beagles chasing the scent of meat

Fear an Tí = master of ceremonies

Flaking the lard out of = thumping

Folly taw = a game of marbles

Glen = short name for Glen Rovers hurling club

Having a stormer = doing well

Keep my powder dry = say nothing for the moment

Kicked the bucket = died

Low Road = lower road, down by Tivoli

Miah's = Miah's was a well-known flea-ridden cinema in Cork long ago. It is now a clothes shop

Mickey dazzler = neatly dressed, shiny clothes, full of colour, and the hair shining, full of oil

Nazareth Home = home for the elderly in Mallow

191

North Infirmary nuns = North Infirmary hospital, run by nuns. It is now an hotel

On song = in great form

Platter face = round fat face

Pucker = Seán Ó Sé had a hit record with 'An Poc ar Buile' and is sometimes referred to as the pucker

Read the riot act = was angry

Roches Point = a lighthouse at the entrance to Cork harbour

Rooley-Booley-Alice = the sky all lit up *[Aurora Borealis]*

Shandon = famous church steeple with four clock faces

St Anns = a famous hurling club on the northside

Such a who began it = a thump

Sullie's Quay School = a school, on Sullivan's Quay, run by the Christian Brothers

Swag = carry or drag

The Banks = short for 'The Banks of My Own Lovely Lee', Cork's anthem

The Blue = colour of St Finbarr's Hurling and Football club

Tóstal = festival celebrated in the 1950s

Up the walls = irritated, anxious

Viaduct = huge railway bridge, spanning the valley beyond Bishopstown on the way to Bandon